Game Dev Stories

Game Dev Stories

More Interviews about Game Development and Culture

Volume 2

David L. Craddock

CRC Press
Taylor & Francis Group
Boca Raton London New York

CRC Press is an imprint of the
Taylor & Francis Group, an **informa** business

First edition published 2022
by CRC Press
6000 Broken Sound Parkway NW, Suite 300, Boca Raton, FL 33487-2742

and by CRC Press
2 Park Square, Milton Park, Abingdon, Oxon, OX14 4RN

CRC Press is an imprint of Taylor & Francis Group, LLC

ISBN: 978-1-032-06265-5 (hbk)
ISBN: 978-1-032-06264-8 (pbk)
ISBN: 978-1-003-20145-8 (ebk)

Typeset in Garamond
by SPi Technologies India Pvt Ltd (Straive)

To Mom and Amie.

Table of Contents

Part I
Old-School

Part 2
Ad Hoc

Acknowledgments

Thank you to all of the individuals who gave so generously of their time to talk to me for the multitude of projects I've written over the past several years: David Brevik, Erich Schaefer, Max Schaefer, Stieg Hedlund, Markus "Smaugy" Sundqvist, MunchaKoopas, David D'Angelo, Sean Velasco, Nick "Woz" Wozniak, Ian Flood, Matt Kowalewski, Woolie Madden, Randy Littlejohn, Will Binder, Isla Schanuel, American McGee, Jennell Jaquays, David Bamberger, Chris Ansell, Brian Harvey, Nate Fox, Lindsey Williamson Christy, Jeff Tangsoc, Joey Godard, and Kevin Regamey.

Thank you to Jason Chen and Simon Carless, the curators of Story Bundle's game development books, for another opportunity to share in the company of so many talented writers.

A huge thank-you to Asif Khan, CEO of Shacknews, for supporting my efforts to chronicle the gaming industry's history.

Last but never least, thank you to my mom, and my wife, Amie, who deserve more praise for their love, support, and encouragement than I will ever be able to give them.

About the Author

David L. Craddock lives with his wife, Amie Kline-Craddock, in Canton, Ohio. He is the author of over two dozen nonfiction and fiction books, including the bestselling *Stay Awhile and Listen* series chronicling the history of Blizzard Entertainment, and *The Gairden Chronicles* series of epic fantasy novels. Follow David online at davidlcraddock.com, facebook.com/davidlcraddock, and @davidlcraddock on Twitter.

Introduction
Introduction

A year consists of 12 months. I assume you know this. Here's something you may not know.

During every one of those months, I spend countless hours conducting interviews with people in the games industry: programmers, artists, marketers, writers. How many hours? You don't know, do you? You can't, because I don't either.

Let's ballpark it: A lot. A lot of hours.

Once I write the articles or books for which I conducted those interviews, the transcripts just sort of sit there, taking up space on my hard drive. Waste not, want not, yes? Yes.

In 2017, I collected some of my favorite interviews and packaged them as *Game Dev Stories: Interviews about Game Development and Culture*. The purpose of the book was to showcase some of the conversations I've had about how games are made and the industry's culture. I also wanted to highlight individuals other than the usual parade of programmers and artists on development teams as a way of showing how many people go into a game's production: marketers, psychologists, writers, and other talented individuals who don't get nearly enough time in the sun.

Game Dev Stories Volume 2: More Interviews about Game Development and Culture was curated in that same vein. In this book, you'll read my conversations with teachers, speedrunners, marketers, and directors. You'll hear from the occasional programmer, too, but the highlights are the folks who deserve as much credit, if not more, for making the magic that made so many of your favorite games magical.

As with *Volume 1*, I've organized the interviews according to topics. Part 1, Old-School, covers games now considered retro, and new games designed with old-school mechanics in mind. Part 2, Ad Hoc, introduces you to individuals who seized opportunities to push the industry forward.

Happy reading!
David L. Craddock

Part I

Old-School

1

David Brevik
Co-Founder of Blizzard North

Readers know me best for *Stay Awhile and Listen*, my trilogy of books on the history of Blizzard Entertainment, Blizzard North, and their franchises, specifically *Diablo*. *Stay Awhile and Listen: Book II—Heaven, Hell, and Secret Cow Levels* was published in the summer of 2019. I've been interviewing Blizzard developers and researching these companies and games for over ten years, and there's still work to be done.

For the first time, I've peeled off extracts from those interviews to publish them in their entirety. Here, David Brevik shares his earliest experiences in the games biz.

**

Craddock: What were some of your earliest experiences playing games?

David Brevik: Probably *Pong*. I don't think that *Pong* was really the cat's meow for me, but by the time my friends and I were playing things like *Space Invaders, Asteroids, Pac-Man*, and stuff like that. There was a sandwich shop, Blimpie, that had a couple arcade machines. There was a place across the street, a pizza place, that had a couple arcade machines as well. We'd go to those places and play. A few of my friends at that point had pinball machines, which I really enjoyed. That was part of my introduction [to video games], and at the same time we had an Atari 2600, and that's what really got me into gaming. *Adventure* was one of my favorites.

I loved *Space Invaders, Pac-Man*, and *Adventure*—those three are some of the first games I remember playing. But really, one of my first experiences with computers… I think it was in the fifth grade, maybe in 1979 or something like that. Somebody at the school had bought an Apple II+ and had it at school. I remember that being a big deal for me. That was really influential.

[Sierra On-Line adventure game, *The Wizard and the Princess*]. I played that game. There was only a monochrome monitor, so it didn't even have any color. It was all green, and there were pages in which there were a couple puzzles. You'd type in "Pick up rock," you know, typing in the sentence, and you could type "List" to get your inventory of six objects that you could hold. Also around that time was the movie *Tron*; that was really influential to me. The graphics that were in [*Tron*] were amazing for the time, things that only a supercomputer could make because of their resolutions. They could render these pictures, it would take maybe a whole day to render one of these images, but to see that in a movie, they could play it back rapidly. I always wanted to make graphics like that.

There were a lot of factors like that that were influential, but most of all it came down to *Pac-Man, Asteroids, Adventure*—all those games were really huge with me.

I was a big Dungeons & Dragons fan. My friends and I would stay up for many late nights. This is right around the time of *Pac-Man, Asteroids*, that stuff. We'd play those games or we'd play D&D—that's pretty much all we'd do. We'd sit down in my friend's basement and play D&D. I have fond memories of those times. We'd paint lead figures and stuff like that.

Craddock: Did you want to make games even then, or were you just a kid having fun?

David Brevik: Making games was absolutely my intention. I think that shortly after discovering the Apple II+ in fifth grade, my dad was leasing computers, and because of that connection, he was able to get an Apple II+ and bring it home. I think that was probably around seventh grade, somewhere in there. That was really the catalyst for me developing as a programmer. I taught myself the Basic language. Around that time you could buy magazines like *Apple Insider* that published articles about how to make games. It would have the code for a complete game inside these magazines. So I would spend hours and hours typing code, and I didn't even know how to type, I was hunting and pecking. But I spent hours and hours typing in the code to run some stupid little game. You couldn't really do much, but I was crazy about these things. Through that process, I was slowly typing these things in—and I mean slowly—and learning what it is that's kind of going on.

Invariably, there were always print errors, bugs, in the code. The games, first off, were kind of throwaway little articles that people would write for these magazines, so they were always buggy. I'd want to modify it, so I had to learn how they worked in order to debug the code, because there was no such thing as a debugger at this time. Through this process of being able to start to learn Basic, start to learn how programming works, learning to debug without a debugger—which benefitted me throughout my career—and understand how things are processed... it was just great.

Then experimenting within that and stretching from learning Basic to learning Assembly. Because the magazines would sometimes have Assembly routines that they would use, like Peek and Poke and stuff like that. There were numbers I could convert, you know, there were decimal numbers I could concert into hexadecimal and I could look them up on a table and see what the instructions were. I could write out the code by hand and follow what they were trying to do. I was learning basically through magazines. They had ads from Bit Brothers or something like that. They were old-fashioned ads that had these guys with moustaches and there were these pieces of code that were maybe ten lines long that would do crazy things like make your computer beep in some kind of rhythm or make a bunch of lines crisscross on the screen.

Eventually I started understanding how all these things worked, and I wanted to do this [for a living]. I started high school in eighth grade. We had all sorts of ancient computers in the math lab in high school: a computer with no CRT; it was a printer, like a typewriter and computer combined into one with a scroll of paper. They called that "letter quality" back then. It would jam and the whole nine yards. They had a punch card machine; they had some really ancient computers there. I was able to learn a little PDP-11 assembly language at that time. My math teacher was helping me out. There were some games. I'd play Lunar Lander. You type in your thrust, and you had variables that told you where you were trying to get, and you had to put in the right numbers; as you put in the thrust you'd get fuel and you had to balance everything to successfully land on the surface of the moon. I'd sit there and try to guess how fast or slow I'd crash, or if I'd land safely.

I'd sit at home and play a lot of games. Things were readily available. I had a 300 baud modem, and I'd call up BBSs and download hacked versions of game and stuff. That was very common. My friends would have shoeboxes full of games on floppy disks and we'd swap them. I bought some games, too, but I couldn't afford everything. I remember one of my favorite games I bought early in that time was *Wizardry*. I bought *Ultima I* through *IV*.

By the time I was in ninth grade I could write my own games. When I was a freshman in high school, I spent a long time making a BMX bicycle game. It used the paddle available for Apple II. The bike would come across the screen, go down hills, go over jumps. You'd press the button to bunny hop, and you had to make jumps and stuff to get to the end. The game could scroll, too. I sent that off to be published in *Apple Insider* magazine. So I knew at the time that this was a passion: I wanted to make games and I wanted to put them out there. I was very serious about it even at a young age, as a freshman in high school.

Diablo (1997).

Craddock: Were you studying games as you played them?

David Brevik: I was sort of a designer, but that wasn't really my passion. It was programming. Trying to make fancy graphics, trying to make things run fast, look good, play well—those were always very critical to me. It wasn't necessarily about game design, it was about making things happen, and the revelation of colors coming into play. I mean, 16 colors—oh my god!

Craddock: Many fans know *Diablo* was influenced in large part by your love of roguelike games. How did you discover those games?

David Brevik: I didn't play very many roguelike games until college. [Attended California State University.] The idea for *Diablo* came about when I was in high school. In fact, I named the game when I was in high school. I lived at the base of Mount *Diablo*. That's where I got the name from. I didn't know any Spanish when I came to the Bay Area. Then I came out here and took a Spanish class in high school, and one day I was like, "*Diablo* means devil. That's awesome!"

I'd write these design documents and I'd title them "*Diablo*." So I really started to get into design—numbers and balance and stuff—around my sophomore or junior year of high school. I started to not only be very interested in programming, but also in design. It wasn't really about critiquing other designs; it was about innovating and creating something very different. Then, of course, I would violate my own rule by playing games that had a massive influence on things that I would do.

I went to college and they had UNIX machines there. And the Internet! This was 1986, so the Internet was just a mess at this time. It was basically schools hooked up to military facilities—basically a fancy Blizzard South that was always connected. You could go to other school's pages and peruse their directories, and they'd have public areas where you could upload things and stuff like that. That's what gave me access to playing games like *Rogue* and *Moria*—games that had random levels, a town, things like that. They were an influence on me as a gamer and ultimately on *Diablo*. I enjoyed these games so much. I spent hours spent on these things.

These old UNIX systems didn't have arrow keys or anything like that. You moved around with HIJK, I think. Then casting spells used M for magic, B for book, and other keys to cast spells, then where you want to target. So you end up wiggling your fingers around typing, and it almost felt like you were casting spells, like "I'm moving around and doing these arcane gestures!" It was this visceral feel, and I always enjoyed that. It doesn't translate to a wide audience, but I always enjoyed that mechanic of typing in what spell you're casting and doing these sort of gestures for different spells. I never made it in any game I've ever done and I doubt I ever will, but I always found it very enjoyable.

So I think those games, ultimately, I knew they were extremely addictive. There were a bunch of people in the lab playing them over and over and over. I spent many hours, pretty much my entire college career, playing roguelike games. I knew before that, I mean, I knew in high school that I wanted to make games. I knew exactly what I wanted to do with my life. I didn't want to do anything else, and I wasn't really interested in anything else. In fact I was barely interested in reading or… I mean, almost anything else in my life wasn't as important as anything that had to do with games or computers. Which kind of hurt me in some ways and helped me in some ways. I became really good at computers and programming. I understood how it worked and could write many things.

In my senior year of high school I was teaching a programming class because I knew C and the teacher didn't. So there was this graduation of my abilities. So I'm not upset where I'm at, but sometimes I wish I had a larger vocabulary, or that I'd just been more well-rounded at that time. But I am who I am.

By the time I left college I knew that I wanted to make [*Diablo*], and I knew that that was… I had a few game ideas, and *Diablo* was one of them, and was probably the most fleshed out, the one I'd realized the most and spent the most time on. I knew that I would be given a chance to do this eventually, but I didn't have the money, knowledge, or contacts to do it quite yet. I had to get my feet wet. I went to college because… See, in high school I was working for Pacific Bell doing telecommunications software, doing modem coding and things like that. And I knew that I didn't actually have to go to college to do what I was already doing proficiently. I could skip college if I wanted and make games right out of high school, or even work for Pac Bell and do a variety of things that I wanted to do.

Unfortunately, or maybe fortunately, I had kind of a baby face syndrome. I looked like I was maybe ten years old by the time I was seventeen. I was skinny, I was baby-faced, I was just this very youthful-looking kid, and because of that people didn't take me seriously. So because of that, I was like, "I'm going to go to college, and I'm going to grow some facial hair, dammit!" And I'm glad that I did. I'm glad I went to school and took the time to do those things. In the end it was really what I needed to do and it helped me immensely, but I was pretty confident at the time that I didn't need it. I was positive I could make money without it. But I experienced things in college like roguelike games that really had a massive impact on where I ended up.

Craddock: What was your plan after finishing school?

David Brevik: Right out of college, I wanted to make games. My parents weren't super-pleased with this decision, but they were fairly supportive. They were hoping I would work for IBM or someplace like that, especially because games weren't the most secure business in the world. This was the Genesis and SNES era. So I said to my parents, "Well, how about I try making games for a little bit? If it doesn't work out, I'll try making your boring-ass spreadsheet programs or something." Those things sounded so boring to me, but I did realize that I needed to pay the bills. I graduated in the spring, then that summer, I got married and had my first job. We were living with my wife's parents at the time. So I was living with her and her family in the San Jose area.

There was an ad in the *San Francisco Chronicle* for a job in San Francisco. Somebody was looking for a game programmer. I took the job at this clipart company called FM Waves. They had less than ten people. They'd focused originally on making clipart. That wasn't working out very well, and they knew the Tramiels, who owned Atari at the time. Through that family connection they were able to get a contract to create a game [*Gordo 106*] for the Atari Lynx handheld. It was about this lab monkey that escapes from an evil scientist. It eventually got released.

In a small world situation, there were two guys who worked at the clipart company, Max and Erich Schaefer. That's where we met. I was a programmer, they were artists. I left, but they stayed on to finish *Gordo 106* and got the rights to do the Super Nintendo version of it. The producer for that company was a guy named Matt Householder who worked for us at Condor, Blizzard, Flagship, et cetera. So there was a connection between the four of us from the early, early 90s.

So I was the programmer on this Atari Lynx game, I'd been working at FM Waves maybe five months or so when my paychecks started bouncing. Definitely didn't want to tell Mom and Dad. It would have brought on the "I told you so" speech. So I knew it wasn't going to work out, and it was time to look for something else more secure, but I still wanted to do video games. I looked in the paper and there was an ad for a new company in Santa Clara. I was living in San Jose, so I was like, "Shorter commute, and my paychecks have a better chance of clearing—in theory."

Craddock: Between FM Waves and Condor, you worked at Iguana. How'd you land there?

David Brevik: So it was another little startup. I was employee number one, I believe. All the other guys were founders—two programmers and two artists. I was the first non-owner. And that was Iguana. My first project there was to convert an arcade machine that Midway was making called *Super High Impact Football* to the Sega Genesis. I did that in three months. There was an artist doing the art but I was the only coder. We finished it and it was one of the first on-time, on-budget projects that Acclaim had had in years. They were very happy with our results. The people doing the Super Nintendo version couldn't get it done; it was a total disaster. We were eventually asked to help out with that. I don't remember if we helped out or not.

Because of that project, we opened the doors for other possibilities. The owner of the company was a guy named Jeff Spangenberg. We started to grow and moved out of our facility and began doing multiple projects. Did some Super Nintendo games. We developed our own dev kits and had our own development machine and our own compiler/assembler. All the games were written in Assembly language at the time. We wrote all the debuggers and everything. Nintendo and Sega didn't provide those things; you had to make your own. They'd give you the hardware specs and say, "Good luck!"

Iguana was going really well. I became the Technical Director there and we were doing all sorts of projects. In fact, Acclaim and Midway wanted us to do a project. Jeff Spangenberg came to me and said, "We did such a good job on *Super High Impact [Football]*, Midway want us to try converting another arcade machine. We're going to go down to the arcade and play the game, it's this new game that just came out. I want to see what you think of it and whether or not you want to do this project." So we went down to the Golfland in Sunnyvale, California, this world famous location to try out arcade games. We played the game, and I was like, "Oh my god, Jeff, this game kicks ass. This is going to be a huge monster hit. We've got to do this game." He said, "Eh, I don't know. I don't really like it that much. It's too weird. It's just this cheap knockoff of another game." I said "Okay, well, I really think it could be awesome." That game was *Mortal Kombat*.

So they came back to us with another arcade machine they wanted us to convert. We went to Golfland and played that one. Again I told Jeff, "This game kicks ass, we've got to do this one." This time he said, "Okay, okay!" That was *NBA Jam*.

NBA Jam on Sega Genesis.

Craddock: What caused you to leave Iguana and start Condor with Max and Erich?
David Brevik: Around the time we started *NBA Jam*, we weren't very far along and Jeff got married. His wife was from Texas so he moved the company to Texas. I didn't want to go. So I left and called up Max and Erich and said, "So, uh, you guys doing anything? Want to start a company?"

"I've got a lot of contacts because I made this game [*NBA Jam*] for Acclaim. I know some guys there." And I knew people over at Sunsoft because we did some work for them such as *Aero the Acro-Bat* and a few other games. I've got contacts there, at Acclaim—I'm sure we can get something. So they said, "Sure, why not? But why don't you help us finish the Super Nintendo version of *Gordo 106*." I'm like, "Eh… not really interested. Call me back when you want to do something different." A couple months later, Max and Erich called me. They said, "Let's do this." We created our own company, and that was Condor.

2

Max and Erich Schaefer
Co-Founders of Blizzard North

This chapter concludes my interview extracts with David Brevik and Max and Erich Schaefer—or "the three bosses" as they were known to the team at Blizzard North—that comprised a generous portion of the material I used to write the *Stay Awhile and Listen* series of books.

A bit of trivia: I structured these interview extracts identically to how I structured the first two chapters of *Stay Awhile and Listen: Book I*. Chapter 1 followed Dave Brevik, and Chapter 2 introduced readers to the Schaefer brothers. I doled out information in that way to give readers time to know all three developers leading up to their auspicious meeting at FM Waves, the company where they daydreamed of one day founding a studio of their own.

**

Craddock: What were some of your earliest experiences playing games?

Erich Schaefer: My first was almost certainly *Pong*. My parents had brought home this weird dedicated console *Pong* game. That's the first I really remember. All it played was *Pong*. [My parents] didn't encourage or discourage [gaming]. I got much deeper into gaming when they brought home an Apple II computer. That's when I played a lot of *Wizardry* and the first Ultimas and stuff like that. I think they thought it was weird that I spent so much time with them, but they didn't discourage.

We definitely played D&D. This was my young teen years back in the '70s and '80s. We didn't play that much D&D. I actually spent more time on my own just making maps and reading the books. Most of my friends just weren't all that interested. They would be willing to play a little bit, but the group I ran around with wasn't that big into D&D. I was the biggest geek in the group and trying to get them to play. But I didn't mind. I just liked the rules, making maps, and designing campaigns, even when I was a little kid. At the time I never considered it as a career. It didn't even enter my mind.

But then later, in my late teens and then through college and even after college, I didn't play any kind of games not all—not console, not arcade, not D&D, none of that, really. But then, kind of in my late 20s when I got back into the game business, definitely all that old stuff kind of came back to me. So I got back into gaming and then into video game design and production at about the same time.

I suspect a few guys were making good money off the hobbyist market. Starting with Lord British on the *Ultima* stuff, he was probably making good money even back then. But it just never occurred to me at all. Definitely not like today where they have school programs. They barely had computers at my school.

Max Schaefer: We'd go to Westwood [California] specifically to hang out in arcades. It was a booming time for them. The arcade was a cool place to be. People had their quarters lined up on the machine. It was a fun time. I'm thinking back to the games that we really liked to play, and we didn't really focus on one. We kind of went from one to another, so whatever was hot at the time, whether it was *Missile Command* or *Galaga* or whatever… probably the one I got best at was *Karate Champ*. That was also a fairly… it was a very direct game. There wasn't a lot of strategy or memorizing or anything. It was a guy beating up on another guy. I think we always appreciated a game design unfettered by many decorations: I never wanted to read a story, I never wanted to remember who was saying what later on—I wanted to play games.

I wouldn't say we were fanatical about it [playing video games], but we were into them. Then we got the home computer, and that kind of really opened up the gaming world for us. We were kids, and we were dumb, so we didn't pay for very much. We certainly played a lot of games; let's just say that. We played some tabletop Dungeons & Dragons as well. Again, not as fanatics by any stretch, but just as enthusiasts. In fact, I would say—it's kind of funny—I would say our D&D game pretty closely mirrored what *Diablo* was like. It was all about getting right into killing skeletons and finding loot. We weren't too focused on lore or rules or anything. It was all about killing monsters and finding good stuff. Erich would usually DM. They were pretty much short attention span theater: getting right to the killing.

I think it definitely had an impact later on with what we wanted to do with making games. Which was absolutely [far from] our minds at the time. We never intended to go into a career of making computer games, even through college. The notion just never hit. It wasn't something you thought about as a career, really.

Craddock: What sorts of things did you like to do besides play games?

Erich Schaefer: Max is around a year and a half younger. We're 16 months apart. Growing up, we had a close but often adversarial and violent relationship. We fought all the time. We had mostly the same friends we'd hang around with. I was much more into Dungeons & Dragons and that kind of things than he was, and we [friends] definitely roped him into those games. I don't think he liked it because he was the younger guy so he kind of got picked on as well as being forced to play a game he didn't like. But we were pretty close, even though we were contentious growing up. We often did the same things: had the same friends, played the same sports.

Max Schaefer:　I was the younger brother, so I was always picked on no matter what we were doing, and kids are unfailingly cruel, so it would often become Erich's point to enrage me. Which I would oblige, of course. I should point out: he was always a foot and a half taller than me, and outweighed me by about 50 pounds growing up. That's not really the case anymore. Once we got into high school, everything kind of evened out. It got pretty funny at times. But it was all in fun, all the typical "big brother, little brother" stuff.

I did piano lessons for five years and was in the school band and stuff. But not very seriously. We played a lot of sports. We were fairly active, outdoorsy kids, I would say. Almost every day we were outside playing sports. And we lived right near the beach, so it was sort of a surfer vibe in the town at the time, and our summers were consumed with going to the beach. It's kind of strange: we didn't have any particular main creative focus. We were particularly poor artists. My dad was a physicist, and my mother was in real estate, so there wasn't a lot of artistic stuff going on. We were math and science students for the most part.

Gordo 106 running on Atari Lynx.

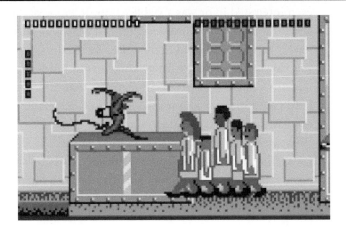

Craddock:　Did your interest in D&D when you were kids make you think about developing games for a living?

Erich Schaefer:　Right out of college I started to do computer graphics stuff. Desktop publishing and business cards and menus and stuff, just because I was handy with computers and could make some decent money on my own doing stuff. While I was goofing around—I think this was on one of the early Macintosh models—I started to learn how to program in C just as a hobby. The first thing I did was start making little arcade games. I think the first one I made was called *Death Balls*. It had bouncing balls and you'd shoot them from below almost like a *Space Invaders* fashion. The balls would get lower and lower and you'd have to blast them away. I think that was my first. It was actually pretty fun. And I think it did start my mind thinking about game design. No one ever played it besides me and a couple of friends, but I started thinking, "You know, I can actually make games."

It took forever because I was learning to code while I was doing it. Sometimes it'd take me a week to figure something out. It wasn't like you could just look these things up. I'd have to go to bookstores and find programming books to help me out. I really had no one to help me. So it took forever, but I just kept modifying it. When it was done I just kept making new kinds of balls that'd jump out, just kept adding on.

For a while I was going to film school, but that was mostly because I failed out of mathematics and programming, and I thought [film] would be an easy degree. I think I've always been creative, and computers were a way to channel my creativity. I can't draw or anything, but I can make art on the computer. I'm a creative guy; I always have been. But I didn't have the drawing talent, or musical talent or anything to get anything going until the computer came around.

Max Schaefer: No. I think we did a little bit of super basic programming, just from scratch, but never really followed up on it. And like I say, it was never really in our minds that making games was something we were really even interested in or was a viable career. It was very early in the industry and for some reason it just never really dawned on us. I don't know that it held much interest for us at the time. We liked to go play football, so sitting down late into the evening banging our heads against a computer—it wasn't something we ever chose to do. That came later. We were dumb kids. Good in math and science, but for some reason not very driven to extracurricular activities that much.

Craddock: What were your first steps into making games?

Max Schaefer: I was in college for four and a half years, so I took the extra semester, mostly due to the shift in majors. We came back home at Christmastime and lived at home for a few months, trying to figure out what we were going to do before we moved in with a couple of friends into [San Francisco] in an apartment, and that's basically where we set up our business.

Erich Schaefer: I think I was living in my mom's basement after college, and then Max graduated from college. His graduation present was a Macintosh computer.

Max Schaefer: I was hoping for a car. I was thinking, "Cool, I'm going to graduate, and my parents will buy me a car. That will be awesome." I unwrapped a computer, and that was pretty awesome too, I thought. Little did I know how awesome it would be. I don't know if Erich mentioned this, but for a good while after college there was three of us who made our living on that one machine.

Erich Schaefer: Neither of us were doing anything or had any real plans of what to do, so we started to get local jobs through people my parents knew, and started to advertise graphics and desktop publishing work, which we did on his computer. In fact there was an old friend of ours, we used to be roommates. The three of us lived together, and lived off of just making art with that one computer for a long time.

Max Schaefer: At the time the business was making logos, brochures, business cards, and that sort of thing for people. With the Mac, it was shockingly easy to do. And yet for a lot of people, it was something they thought was rocket science. Those people just hadn't had the exposure to computers and the programs, and how easy it was to do. So we found a lot of business, enough to keep us able to buy beer.

It was a couple of friends, but only one of the friends participated in the business with us. His name is Craig, and our company was called Desktop Heroes; we did desktop publishing. Yes, [shared one Mac computer], which kind of goes to show our work ethic at the time. There was plenty of computer to go around! A lot of the time you're out running around talking to clients or showing them stuff, and so there was plenty of time for whoever needed to be on the computer to be using it. I don't recall [any of us saying], "Hey, there's only one machine. This isn't working."

Running a business like Desktop Heroes, doing freelance logo design and brochure stuff, you had to spend a lot of time on business, mostly finding clients. That wasn't something that any of us had a particular talent for or a desire to spend a lot of time on. At some point we decided, "Hey, there's this organization called Mac Temps"; they paid fairly well at the time, and would send you off to companies to make brochures and logos and stuff. So we thought, rather than hustling business ourselves, we'll just go in to these guys and have them send us to work wherever. So we started doing that, and that provided more steady hours. It led to me getting a position at FM Waves.

Craddock: How did the job at FM Waves lead you to Dave Brevik?

Max Schaefer: FM Waves was making clipart at the time, and I was hired to make borders for people to put on their brochures. It was basically sitting at the computer, using Adobe Illustrator, and making border after border after border. They had a bunch of other work they were putting together, too. Eventually my brother got hired on as well, and our friend Craig also spent a little time there.

Erich Schaefer:	The guy who owned FM Waves—it was a pretty small operation; my brother, me, a couple other guys—the guy who owned this company got a contract through his dad to make an Atari Lynx video game. That was the big start. So the owner said, "Hey, you've got to make art for this video game." And I had no clue what that meant. So we had to make it all up from scratch. At the same time the owner hired David Brevik, a programmer right out of college who was interested in making games. He was the programmer of this game. So it was David Brevik, Max, and me making this game called *Gordo 106.* So that's how we got started making games. Just kind of by accident.
Max Schaefer:	It was really a complete coincidence that the owners were our age. They were a couple of nice guys, but they were definitely trying to set up a business using their dad's money. It wasn't a rigorously professional organization, just a couple of guys trying to set up a business. For whatever reason, through family connections or whatever, they got contracts to make a video game for the Atari Lynx, and that was basically our start in the video game industry. It came as an assignment from them. They were like, "Hey, we have this opportunity to make a game, so we're going to hire a programmer, and you guys should do the art for it." And we thought that sounded pretty cool, like a fun job to do. So we got this contract and started into it, and a light bulb definitely went on; it was like, "Okay, yeah, this is what we want to do for our careers." It was obviously fun, it was something we could definitely do, and we could see how to do it better than anyone else was doing. It was completely unintentional, but when it happened, it was obviously the right thing; finally, we'd figured out what we were going to do for a career.
Erich Schaefer:	And it came out pretty good. The game was fun. It came out right at the end of the Lynx cycle, which wasn't very [long] anyway; there was probably a very limited amount of people who played or even saw this thing. But the three of us, Max and Dave and I, we all knew that video games were the thing for us. It's fun, we can do it, and that's what we should pursue.
Max Schaefer:	So we started to put together this game, and it was obviously fun, and it was obviously competitive. You could look at what we were doing, and look at what other people were doing, and say, "Yeah, we can actually do this." It was right about then that FM Waves bounced a check, and Dave was gone. That was the beginning of the end of FM Waves. They ran out of money. Brevik left because he'd just gotten married and was having a kid; he couldn't really afford to have checks balancing. We were slackers living in an apartment with friends and zero expenses, so we didn't really care. We kept at it just to see where it would go. We brought in a substitute programmer, and he was kind of a crazy guy. We struggled through making the rest of the game, but the game did end pretty much when we finished the game.

Diablo.

Erich Schaefer:	FM Waves went out of business shortly after that. Even before that, Dave left and joined Iguana. When FM Waves crashed, they just gave us all the computer equipment that we'd been working with. So we started another little company, Atomic Games, I believe. That was Max, me, and a couple either guys working with us, but that didn't work out that well.
Max Schaefer:	Basically, toward the end of it, when it was obvious that it wasn't going to work out with this guy and the project wasn't going to go anywhere, we called up Brevik and asked, "What are you doing? Let's get our own company going. Let's make something happen." And David was working at Iguana Entertainment at the time. I guess when I called him, he was sitting next to his boss, so he said, "No. I'm happy here. Everything's going great. Not interested. Good luck, guys. Keep in touch." So that was that.

I found out later that he was actually sitting next to his boss when I'd called, which was kind of why [our phone conversation] went that way. But also that they [Iguana] were planning on moving the company to Austin, Texas. Dave didn't want to go to Texas at all, so a couple months later, he called and said, "Hey, are you guys still interested?" And I remember I'd had several beers that night when he called. And I was like, "Uh, yeah, I think we are. Yeah, absolutely. Let's talk about it in the coming days." He told us the story of how [Iguana] was moving to Texas and he didn't want to live in Texas, and was willing to quit even though they were doing pretty cool stuff. We decided pretty much right then, "Yeah, we're going to do this. Let's have a meeting."

Erich Schaefer: Back at FM Waves when Dave, Max, and I worked together for the first time, we would say, "Hey, we shouldn't make games for these guys. We should go make games on our own." We referred to it around the office as Project: Condor. That was our codeword for starting our own thing. Shortly after creating Condor—in fact, at our very first meeting—we got a phone call from somebody who used to work with David on the *Aero the Acro-Bat* project. Called us up out of the blue at our first meeting and said, "Hey, we want you to make games for us." Within a couple of weeks we had a contract, got an office, and started to make a legit business.

We went to Dave's house and discussed how we were going to make a company. During that very first meeting, the phone rang, and it was one of the publishers that he'd worked with at Iguana. They'd heard he'd left and they said, "Hey, if you're starting up something new, we've got lots of games we need to make." So in our first organizational meeting for the new company, which was Condor, we had an offer to pick from a list of games to make. It was really good synchronicity. During our initial discussion, the phone rings, and we've got work. It was one in a series of really lucky things that happened to us along the way.

3

Stieg Hedlund
Designer on Diablo *and* Diablo II

Within the walls of Blizzard North, *Diablo's* developers referred to monsters by internal pet names. A favorite among the team was the hidden, known internally as the sneaky demon. It lived up to its moniker. Tall and well-built, the sneaky demon cloaks itself in invisibility as it moves toward the player. It appears in a haze, like heat rising from a fire, and then attacks, dealing tremendous damage with its claws.

Stieg Hedlund shares much in common with the sneaky demon. He's no monster, and he's not sneaky, but the experienced designer joined Blizzard North late in *Diablo's* development—almost out of thin air—and immediately set to balancing the game to the high degree of polish it needed to become a success when it launched a few months later. He was the newest member, yet his aptitude for design and balance was so far-reaching he may as well have been there all along, hiding, waiting to emerge and *hack* and slash the *hack*-and-slash into shape.

In a way, Stieg had been there all along. He was among the first to interview for a job at Blizzard North back when it had started as a small, three-developer studio called Condor, Inc., but declined an offer. Part of my time interviewing Stieg Hedlund for my *Stay Awhile and Listen* books was spent learning more about his prolific background in game design, why he initially rejected Condor's offer, and what finally brought him into the fold. I present that interview in full below, taken from its original publication on *Stay Awhile and Listen: Book II's* Kickstarter in the summer of 2018.

**

Craddock:	Your entry on Wikipedia states that you became a pen-and-paper RPG designer by the age of 16. What led to your interest in RPGs, both playing and designing them?
Stieg Hedlund:	I got the Basic D&D boxed set as a gift pretty much as soon as it came out. I essentially collected war games at that time in my life; I already had some of Steve Jackson's stuff, like *Ogre*, as well as Avalon Hill

games like *Panzer Blitz*. I couldn't always get someone to play with me, but I would pore over rulebooks and run scenarios in my head for hours. The amateurish illustrations were hard to get past at first, but actually reading it, it still stuck in my mind as pretty awesome, so I convinced some family members to play. I think that was the last time I looked at that version of the game, because I went out and bought the advanced rulebooks and AD&D almost immediately became all-consuming for me.

Just as later in electronic games, I was not content to merely play a character in someone else's world: I started thinking about my own worlds, delving into alternate character classes, rule sets, and looking at how to present the type of experience I was interested in. After a while, all the research, math, and storytelling seemed to reach a critical mass where just sharing it with my friends was kind of a waste, so I started looking at ways to expand my audience, as well as getting paid. The direction that they were moving towards for 2nd edition seemed to be moving toward complexity in order to solve the balance issues of the 1st edition, which I saw as a major mistake, so I went away from it in the mid to late '80s.

Craddock: Making games professionally sounds like it was a natural step for you, then. How did you get your start in the industry?

Stieg Hedlund: I worked for one of the first desktop publishing places to come into being—a place right by UC Berkeley—and one of our customers ran an early game publisher called Infinity. He needed computer-savvy people, and hired me and a couple of my friends. I wore a whole bunch of hats, but with a focus on testing and tech support, but the actual development was all out of house. Also the place fell apart—the developers promised deliveries, and we took them at their word, made big ad buys, and then had nothing to sell. The company started having trouble making payroll, people started leaving, and it became a downward spiral. It was kind of a capsule of how things often go in the games business, and taught me a lot of lessons about what not to do, if nothing else.

I was constantly playing games both as part of my job at Infinity and on my own and knew I wanted to make them. I had always been good at art, attending the School of the Art Institute of Chicago after high school, and looking at the artwork in games, I knew I could do better than ninth-tenths of what I was seeing, so I looked at art as a potential way in for those who couldn't see my pen-and-paper experience as bona fides for electronic gaming.

Die Hard Arcade.

Craddock:	What led to your position at Koei Corporation?
Stieg Hedlund:	When I was looking around for an artist position in the Bay Area, they had recently relocated from Southern California, and were looking to staff up, and they were looking for their first game artist. They hired me and sent me to Japan. Since their main operation was there, it was their practice to send the people they hired in the US over to be trained.

Koei had managed some good successes in Japan at that time, and wanted to get a piece of the North American market as well. They were just starting their first US-directed title, and my manager was heading up the effort. After I got back to the US, he was always running gameplay ideas by me. After I'd only been at Koei for a couple of months, he was wooed away by EA, and recommended me to the Koei management as being able to continue the design. So I took over *Liberty or Death*, a strategy game set in the US War of Independence. Even prior to that, I had proposed a spate of games that leveraged Koei's technology, including an RPG based on the Monkey King that I felt would complete their "set" of games based on classics of Chinese literature. All of the games I proposed got made eventually, though most of them after I'd left, so the results were not what I would've wanted.

In addition to shepherding *Liberty or Death* from pre-alpha all the way to ship, I also proposed Celtic Tales, Gemfire, and Saiyuki: Journey

West, some of which I worked on prototypes for and others that I had no other involvement in beyond the initial design. In addition, I became what was known as a project manager, dealing with both the strategy and day-to-day management of localizing titles from Japan, from design and art to actual translation. I did it all including package design and manual writing, it was pretty crazy. *Liberty or Death* remains one of my proudest achievements, even though it didn't find a huge audience, just because so much of it was me.

I had to really internalize the nuts-and-bolts information of what needs to be done when; since I was working with teams that were on different sides of the world, and what's more email and the Internet were still in their infancy at the time. Communication had to be clear and precise, as well as timely.

Craddock: Many gamers, especially fans of Japanese companies such as Nintendo and Sega, view the games and culture that have permeated the West with a kind of reverence. It becomes a point of pride to have visited or lived in the Land of the Rising Sun. What was it like living and working in Japan?

Stieg Hedlund: I actually lived in Japan for around three years in all, though not in a single continuous chunk. I've been back for work a couple of times, and it's still like a home away from home to me. What was really interesting in Japan, at least at that time, was that people joined companies without any particular expertise, training or, often, talent. They were sort of thrown into the deep end—sink or swim—and even if they sank, that didn't mean they got fired. Instead they became obstacles to those of us who were actually interested in making great games. People moved into management based on coming from good schools as well. And all the things that people here think about how hard the Japanese work is, to put it kindly, PR.

Also, interestingly, no credits were given to the people who worked on the games; instead, all games were attributed either to Kou Shibusawa, or Eiji Fukuzawa, both non-entities, and really a way for the President of Koei to retain credit for the games for himself, despite his having little involvement in the actual development of any of the games.

I wish I could name more positives: people think that game development in Japan is some kind of magical fairyland, and maybe if you work with Miyamoto at Nintendo it is, but apart from meeting schedules way better than any organization I've worked with elsewhere, I found it just as dysfunctional. Similar to US game dev, the heroic efforts of a few passionate and creative individuals are really what made projects come together, in spite of (rather than because of) layers of ignorant and ineffectual middle- and upper management.

This last thing is the key learning I came away with; if I wanted to work on successful games, my own dedication and effort was the main thing I could rely on to make it happen: I had to be disciplined enough to set goals and a cadence for completion in order to get things done to a level that I could be proud of within the timeframes I was given. It is perhaps ironic that in contact with a culture of teamwork, my spirit of independence was sparked.

Craddock: How did you find your way to Condor?

Stieg Hedlund: Condor was just the three founding guys then; Max and Erich Schaefer and Dave Brevik. They were located right by the Redwood City marina in B-grade office space—it was a different part of the same complex they were in when I did join them as Blizzard—a space that was very broken up into odd-sized offices. Stuff was in boxes and they had miscellaneous beat-up desks and chairs. It sounds grim, but it really didn't put me off: when I started there, Koei was in about eight different tiny offices spread around the town of Hiyoshi, and to this day I find overly-nice offices—particularly for startups—a bit suspicious.

Craddock: I find this part of your story especially fascinating: the bosses offered you a job, but you turned it down, only to circle back later. Why didn't the first time work out for you?

Stieg Hedlund: It was tough, honestly. I really liked the Schaefers and Dave, and the feeling must have been mutual, because they did offer me the job. One factor was that I was trying to move into design and away from art, and Acclaim already had the design covered, and it didn't interest me very much artistically either (since it was just matching the comic book's style).

What it really came down to was healthcare. They hadn't gotten around to it, and weren't really sure what they would do about it, and since my wife was in grad school at the time, I needed a job that could provide it.

Craddock: Where did you go after turning down Condor?

Stieg Hedlund: I went to work for Sega Technical Institute, one exit north of Condor on highway 101. STI was kind of an odd place—it offered a lot of great opportunities for those that were self-motivated, and I managed to take advantage of that during my time there. In the roughly three-and-a-half years I was there I shipped three games, as well as contributing to another two (one shipped, and the other didn't) and pitching several more. The ones I completed were *The Ooze, Die Hard Arcade*, and *Comix Zone*.

Another designer had headed up *Comix Zone*, but I was lead on the other two, exploring some very new and unique gameplay in *The Ooze* (which unfortunately didn't receive any type of marketing push, but eventually found favor with retro gamers), and working with guys from Sega's AM2 division to execute an iconic beat-'em-up as well as the first 3D game for both our studios in *Die Hard Arcade*.

Between Koei and Sega, I had also worked as a freelancer for EA, doing both design and art/ animation for an abortive Lord of the Rings-based game for the Sega Genesis called *Ring of Doom*. This experience gave me entree to both Condor and Sega as having more direct application to what they were doing, as well, of course, as the prestige.

Sonic the Hedgehog 2.

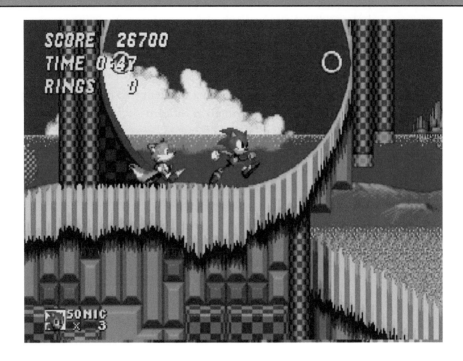

Craddock:	Why did you leave STI?
Stieg Hedlund:	I mentioned the things I accomplished while at STI, but there were also those in the studio who had managed to get absolutely nothing out the door in that time. There were huge management and political issues—particularly around the *Sonic* brand. I had basically learned I had to avoid *Sonic* in order to be successful there.
	Still I could only really help the games that I was assigned to, and by mid '96 the writing was on the wall—there were management shakeups at SOA [Sega of America], and when our general manager was given the well-deserved heave-ho it seemed like I should definitely dust off my resume. And in fact the whole studio was shuttered a few months later, allowing me to hire the few people I thought were worth their salt.
Craddock:	What circumstances brought you back to Condor?
Stieg Hedlund:	I went over there because I was just starting to get my stuff together to begin a job hunt, and couldn't find a portfolio that contained some originals of my artwork. Thinking about when I had seen it last, I determined that I had left it at Condor when I'd interviewed there, and went over to see if they could dig it up. We looked around, but couldn't find it, but they definitely made it clear that they wanted me to join them as well, and we started discussing that.

They showed me around, introduced me to the team—they'd grown to around 20 guys, occupying most of one floor of the office building—and they were definitely excited to have me see *Diablo*.

Craddock: Obviously, you accepted that job. What drew you to the *Diablo* project?

Stieg Hedlund: I had some definite opinions about what was wrong with the CRPGs to that point, and which things worked. I had a bit of a manifesto going—a list of RPG cruft that I thought was really unnecessary, things like die-rolling for character creation, selection of skills prior to experiencing the game world, derivative EDO storylines, playing a party rather than a character, dialogue trees, and so-called moral choices.

When I first saw *Diablo*, it closely jibed with a lot of my thinking about CRPGs. I dug that it took a lot of its cues from *Doom* and *Quake* rather than the D&D-based stuff I'd soured on. I thought *Diablo* needed some polish, but was a game that would be at least popular to warrant a sequel, where I could explore even more of the things I was interested in.

Everything just came together this time around: I was looking to make a change, and I liked what I saw at Blizzard North, and they knew they needed a dedicated designer (as the people who worked on the design for *Diablo* also had art or other duties as their primary roles), they'd already liked me the last time, and I'd stacked a lot more hard-core design production experience since then.

Craddock: Could you expand on the role you played on the original *Diablo*?

Stieg Hedlund: My title was senior designer. As I've mentioned, they wanted someone to be solely responsible for design. For *Diablo*, they wanted someone who could come in and drive down details, getting to a well-polished and -balanced game as efficiently as possible, but they were already looking ahead to other games and wanted to start building a team for the future. I was the guy who could hold and guide the vision of a game and determine which gameplay mechanics and features a game needed.

Matt Householder came on as Senior Producer soon after I joined, and for some of the same reasons: they needed these roles filled to transition from a small company to a "grown-up" game studio.

Craddock: You joined the team fairly late in *Diablo*'s development cycle. How did you go about getting the game polished and balanced?

Stieg Hedlund: There still was a small-company atmosphere during the development of *Diablo*, and I made use of my ability to wear a lot of hats to help nail things down almost wherever that needed to happen, reviewing quest wording, art deliverables from HQ—they produced the item icons—listening to sound files with Matt Uelmen, etc.

Craddock: One comment I've heard time and again during these interviews is that *Diablo* was as fun to play as it was fun to make. What are some of your favorite anecdotes from testing and building the game?

Stieg Hedlund: You know the different portals on the surface that lead to different dungeon levels? That came about because of me, Michio Okamura, and Eric

Sexton. We were playing in a group together and decided that instead of going where we were supposed to, we'd jump into a higher-level dungeon. We were getting killed a ton, sure, but we were also able to level-up really quickly. It was pretty funny because we were yelling and screaming and running back and forth to each other's desks to see what was happening. Pretty soon a lot of people were watching us, and we all determined that we needed to restrict access to dungeons based on character level.

At one point groups of Skeleton Kings, intended to only be a boss monster, started spawning on a level. The same kind of scenario started happening, where we were getting killed a lot, but getting massive XP each time we killed them.

The day after Christmas, they called and asked me to come in and help make sure the last couple of bugs were gone, and I was happy to pitch in, regardless of the holiday. It was great to be there to master it up, and send the gold disks off to be duplicated.

4

Speedy Shovelry
Shovel Knight *Speedrunners*

Shovel Knight by David L. Craddock is the 19th book in publisher Boss Fight Books' series of nonfiction titles about game development and gaming culture, and is available in paperback and digital editions. Due to concerns over page count, a chapter on speedrunning was left on the cutting-room floor. I present that chapter, written from my interviews with the individuals therein, in full below.

**

For every *Mega Man 2* and *Super Mario Bros. 3*, droves of NES sequels failed to capture the spirit of what had made their predecessors fun. *Castlevania II: Simon's Quest*, for instance, had a suitably creepy atmosphere and haunting soundtrack. In retrospect, its gameplay involved tedious item gathering, and its progression is considered esoteric and capricious at best. The third game, however, is considered a classic for improving on the original's central conceits of action and platforming.

Konami and other developers can be forgiven for missing the mark on one sequel only to stick the landing on the next. They had no way to measure what fans liked and what they condemned in an original title until reviews were published weeks or months after release, by which time studios had already committed significant time and resources to a plan for the follow-up. Today, the universality of direct and near instantaneous methods of interaction such as social media and Twitch let developers keep a finger on the pulse of their communities, and plan development of sequels accordingly.

Inviting Kickstarter backers to watch as David D'Angelo programmed Tinker Knight was only one example of how Yacht Club bridged the narrowing gulf between creator and consumer. Their frequent communication with pro players such as Smaugy and MunchaKoopas, two of the fastest *Shovel Knight* speedrunners around, is another, one that continues to send a ripple effect throughout the design of the game's add-on packs. "I think I got under an hour on the original *Shovel Knight* when it launched, or maybe right around an hour. They're running at like forty minutes," D'Angelo said of speedrunners. "They're god tier compared to me. There's no question about it."

Tailoring *Shovel Knight* to speedrunners as well as to casual players was a priority for Yacht Club, for personal and professional reasons. "We try to engage with that speedrunner community because those are the people we are," Velasco said. "I grew up speedrunning *Mega Man 2* and *Super Metroid*, so [speedrunning is] near and dear to me."

"Even if you're not speedrunning it per se, people do try to go through the game quickly," explained D'Angelo. "Say you're replaying it. You say, 'I'm just going to run through this room at full speed because I know this room.' If it isn't fun to run through that room at full speed, it's going to be crappy for someone. I think an average player runs into that a lot, actually. I'm going at full clip in *Mega Man*, and the [enemy] spawns and hits me if I'm going full clip. That ruins the experience. I'm playing the game a lot from that point of view for sure."

Markus "Smaugy" Sundqvist, his online handle adapted from the avaricious dragon Smaug in J. R. R. Tolkien's *The Hobbit*, is one of the *Shovel Knight* community's most well-known speedrunners. He had a background playing competitive e-sports games such as *Counter-Strike 1.6* and *Quake Live* before looking for another type of game on which to leave his mark. "I wanted to get back into something that is both fun and competitive," Smaugy explained. "I had already been watching speedruns from time to time and I loved the amount of time you had to put into it in, how much practice, passion, and dedication you needed to become good. I saw it as a challenge and figured I would try it out and see how good I could become."

Fortuitously, Smaugy developed an interest in speedrunning a few days out from the 2015 *Summer Games* Done Quick. Known as SGDQ, the annual event is a week-long gathering where the best speedrunners in the world blaze through games new and old to raise money for charity. Watching over Twitch, Smaugy happened to catch a speedrunner known as MunchaKoopas playing a retro-style platformer called *Shovel Knight*. MunchaKoopas was playing in the Low% category, a type of race where the player skips optional content in favor of the fastest possible route to the end. Smaugy's eyes widened as he watched MunchaKoopas sprint through the Order of No Quarter and defeat the Enchantress in just shy of 50 minutes.

"*Shovel Knight* reminded me of older games such as *Castlevania*, *DuckTales*, *Mega Man*, *Super Mario*, and *Zelda*," Smaugy said. "So I picked it up, started learning, and I was hooked."

Capcom's *Duck Tales* on NES.

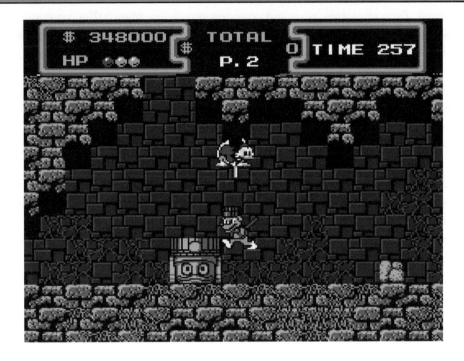

MunchaKoopas followed a similar path to speedrunning, tuning into SGDQs and AGDQs (Awesome Games Done Quick, a winter event) and staring in amazement as donations poured in. "I was amazed that this was a hobby in the first place, and that people were using it to do some good in the world," he said.

MunchaKoopas remained a spectator until 2014, when *Shovel Knight's* launch on PC and Nintendo's Wii U and 3DS systems coincided with the start of SGDQ. "I had the week off work and played while I watched the stream, and I decided it would be my first speed game. I fell in love with the way the game played and all the clever uses the items had. Even the basic shovel can be used to great effect."

MunchaKoopas and Smaugy take different approaches to perfecting their techniques. For MunchaKoopas, practice makes perfect. "People ask me often, 'How long does it take to learn *Shovel Knight?*' I never have an answer because for me it's been an ongoing process of almost three years now," he said.

Smaugy has never played *Shovel Knight* the way casual players do—exploring, returning to the Village to talk to the NPCs, watching the Troupple King and his fishy brigade perform their dance routine. "I wanted to play as much as possible so I could get used to the game, the mechanics of items, physics of jumping, the shovel attacks and the behavior of the enemies," he said. "So I picked up a few new tricks every day and after every personal best I pretty much looked at two to three of my biggest problems at the time and fixed those problems, and then I repeat that cycle."

Speedrunners tend to focus on honing their techniques for certain categories, such as shovel-only runs or 100% competition—meaning no relics left behind, no levels skipped, no bosses unchallenged. Even after three years and countless speedruns, MunchaKoopas is still amazed at just how much can be done with the game's default weapon. "I started running Low%, or shovel only, as my first category," he said. "I worked hard with friends to find techniques to beat the game with only the shovel in under forty-eight minutes. It will forever be my favorite category. The way the shovel interacts with the world around *Shovel Knight* is beautifully crafted."

Smaugy and MunchaKoopas usually stream the game while they play, providing a running commentary that gives viewers insight into their strategies and practice sessions. Before long, both runners noticed one viewer who stood out from the rest.

"One of the members of Yacht Club Games started watching me on a daily basis when I streamed my *Shovel Knight* speed runs, and still [watches]," said Smaugy. "We developed a friendship, and that's how I realized YCG appreciates us speedrunners as we are the ones who know a huge amount of the game and how things work."

"Shane [Calimlim] from YCG has been hanging around *Shovel Knight* speedrun channels since late 2014," added MunchaKoopas. "He has been an amazing friend to me, and I am eternally thankful for everything he has done not only for me but for the community. He has been our voice to the rest of the development team."

Yacht Club's developers appreciated both runners' enthusiasm for the game and extended offers to let them play early builds of patches and expansion packs, such as 2015's *Plague of Shadows* and 2017's *Specter of Torment*, in exchange for providing feedback—on bugs they find, on glitches they exploit, and on the techniques they employ. "When I play an early build, I try to simply enjoy the experience of playing that character or mode for the first time," explained MunchaKoopas. "If I am doing actual testing, I am looking for bugs and small changes. It's mostly to make sure that speedruns still function the same way."

"I'm making sure mechanics are working as usual," said Smaugy. "Items doing what they're supposed to do, looking at if there is any changed behavior in enemies, bosses, or physics. I've been mostly confirming that things are working as intended, what feels good when playing."

Smaugy and MunchaKoopas report bugs or glitches they find while testing. Yacht Club's developers evaluate each one. Some they consider too detrimental to the game's structure and squelch. Others are deemed fun enough to stick around, or so esoteric that casual players have little chance of stumbling over them and botching their progress. Smaugy is credited with discovering a technique that he and the community have coined "Bubble Wrap." It can be performed in the *Plains of Passage*, and saves three to four seconds of time if executed correctly.

"The trick is to do a specific setup to make two bubbles from a dragon shoot up into the sky, and you pogo up on them at a specific moment," Smaugy explained, "and you touch the loading screen of the screen above at the same time as you are touching the screen transition to your left. This trick teleports you up to the screen above which enables you to skip going around the long way."

Some of the glitches that speedrunners report surprise Yacht Club Games. Jump-cancelling was one such. "You could hit an enemy with the shovel drop or with your regular Shovel Blade attack, and then you can go into another attack right after that," Velasco said. "So when an enemy's flashing state is over, your shovel could be inside the enemy, and as long as your hit box is valid they will take another hit. They will use that to do a one-two combo, as it were."

Yacht Club felt compelled to correct jump-cancelling, foreseeing scenarios where the player could intentionally get wedged between the topmost screen border and a tall enemy. If players cannot fall, Shovel Knight's sprite interlocks with the enemy's sprite. Both hit boxes are valid, enabling players to drill the enemy with shovel drops until it dies or the player gets pushed onto the next screen over. Speedrunners urged the team to reconsider. "We tried to make adjustments to hit boxes in some cases," Velasco added, "but they said, 'No, leave it in; this is a cool, extra technique.'"

Yacht Club knew about damage boosting, but left it in the code because they saw it as a technique that savvy players would want to exploit. "I think we just deal with [glitches] on a case-by-case basis," Velasco stated. "If one would make the game look extremely broken, we would take it out. If it's one that only a speed runner would encounter, or has an extremely small chance of being able to happen, we might leave it."

Propeller Knight has a reputation as one of the most difficult bosses for casual players and speedrunners alike. He's quick, spends much of the fight hovering in the air out of reach, and calls in an airship to fire cannonballs. Even MunchaKoopas feared the winged knight—until he figured out a way to defeat him in 19 seconds flat.

For his opening salvo, Propeller Knight lunges back and forth, trying to impale players on his rapier. MunchaKoopas counters by pulling off a series of jump-cancels to score hits on the boss every time he lunges. If employed correctly, Propeller Knight's health bar will be reduced by half. "To make this work the player has to use jump to cancel their ground attack and then face the other direction to hit propeller again," he said. It's a tough trick to learn but it makes the fight incredibly easy.

MunchaKoopas and Smaugy dig into their bag of tricks every time they attempt a speedrun. Early in 2017, the two friends and friendly rivals got a chance to pit their skills against one another in a race at AGDQ. The goal: be the first to finish the game in the Low%, shovel-only category.

Both players took seats before monitors at the front of an auditorium packed with fans and peers. Smaugy and MunchaKoopas were there to have fun and raise money for charity, but Smaugy confessed to feeling pressure. Not only were they in a room full of people, tens of thousands of viewers tune in on Twitch at any given time during the week-long event.

"In races you want to be somewhat safe in the route you are taking to ensure if you die, you won't lose as much time if it does happen," said Smaugy.

Both runners took their time getting settled. MunchaKoopas got a wave of laughter when he removed his headphones to put on a beanie in the shape of *Shovel Knight*'s helmet, then slipped his headset on overtop it. One of the commentators initiated a countdown. "Three, two, one, go!" Cheers and applause broke out as two *Shovel Knights* on two screens broke into a run across the *Plains of Passage*. While they played, another speedrunner versed in *Shovel Knight* provided commentary to explain tricks they performed. MunchaKoopas and Smaugy shut out comments and cheers. They sat forward, eyes glued to their screens. They were in the zone.

MunchaKoopas falls into his zone by treating solo runs at home no differently than live events like AGDQ. "I practice full game runs, individual levels, spots I have trouble with."

"The most important thing to do is get into the mindset of 'I can never stop, no matter what mistakes happen. I have to keep going,'" MunchaKoopas said. "I try to approach it like a musical instrument."

By the time they finished the boss rush and headed into the first of two battles against the Enchantress, Smaugy held the lead by three seconds. Entering the villainess's room, both players threw a chaos orb and batted the Enchantress's projectiles back at her. Both Smaugy and MunchaKoopas took her down within a second of one another. Spectators exploded in applause. Smaugy grinned and wiped sweaty palms on his pants. MunchaKoopas gave a quick nod, not looking away from his screen.

"Coming down to final Enchantress, man," the commentator said, voice shaky. "This is… I'm excited. That's all I can say." He gave a giddy laugh. "That's all I can say."

Smaugy put his game face back on. MunchaKoopas shifted in his chair, sitting up straighter. Shield Knight fell from the top of the screen in dramatic slow-mo. Both players leaped to catch her, as much as to speed things up as out of concern for her wellbeing. In the background, the towering form of the Remnant of Fate faded into view. Her life meter filled. The fight began. As Remnant of Fate unleashed glowing orbs that bounced around the screen, Shield Knight's AI kicked in. She commenced pacing back and forth, leaping up and down the disjointed ground and looking for an opportunity to hold her shield aloft so that players could shovel-drop against it, pogo into the air, and clock Fate's head. When and how often Shield Knight raises her shield depends on RNG, or random-number generation, speedrunner shorthand for an action or event out of their control.

Shovel Knight.

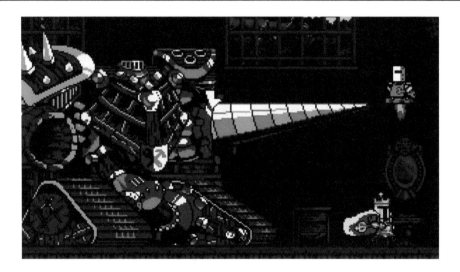

After pogoing against Shield Knight's shield, the trick to beating Remnant of Fate quickly is to bludgeon her head with a series of jump-cancels and shovel drops. Both players encountered difficulty at first; Shield Knight seemed dead set against being helpful, wandering back and forth when both players desperately needed her to jump. Smaugy got lucky when his computer-controlled partner cooperated sooner. He boosted off her shield and carved down the boss's life bar. When the Remnant of Fate scooted to the side—a preprogrammed reflex to prevent players from defeating her too easily—Smaugy took flight after her using the Propeller Dagger and continued his onslaught. His screen began to flash. The Remnant of Fate was down. Smaugy was victorious at 46:10.

"Mentality comes into play as well," explained Smaugy. "If you start doubting a trick you're about to do, you start to think," Oh, no, I might mess this up, don't mess this up. So usually the best thing to do [is to play] as you would in your normal speedrun attempts.

Smaugy tried to stand but got tangled in his headset. "Yeah, but, the cord," he protested.

"Don't worry about it," MunchaKoopas said. Smaugy heeded his mentor and disentangled himself. The two friends embraced, clapping each other on the back and thanking one another for a nail-biter of a race.

The crowd began to break up. MunchaKoopas held up a finger and asked for a few extra moments. He held down buttons to scrub through the game's ending. On the credits screen, he pointed out his name and the names of other speedrunners listed in the special-thanks section, then initiated another round of applause for Smaugy, whose name was given a special shout out.

CURRENT ANY% SPEEDRUN RECORD
SHOVEL KNIGHT
SMAUGY
00:43:51

Sharing the memory still elicits a grin. "It has been an incredible journey throughout my speedrunning and streaming it live to countless people watching me," Smaugy said. "I feel like speedrunning is my home; it has given me much practice and development in my mentality and personality. Spending so many hours playing this has given me an insanely amount of joy and seeing other people coming to ask me [for] advice about the game is a very good feeling. *Shovel Knight* is and will be for a long time one of my favorite games to play and speedrun. For Shovelry!"

MunchaKoopas has won his fair share of races, and lost others. His record does not matter to him. He's just along for the ride.

"After so much time spent playing *Shovel Knight*, I can honestly say that it has become part of my identity," MunchaKoopas said. "My friends outside of speedrunning joke that I lead a double life. I am a shy, reserved person most of the time. At speedrun events I try to be more outgoing and friendly to people. *Shovel Knight* has given me chances to travel the country, raise money for charity, make amazing friends, and even led me to a lovely lady I am rather fond of! I am not sure I will ever stop playing *Shovel Knight*. If I could go back in time and tell 15-year-old me he would be working with a game developer one day, I am certain he would demand a high five. This game has given me a new lease on life and I cannot imagine life without it."

5

Boss Digs
Designing Boss Fights in Shovel Knight

Shovel Knight by David L. Craddock is the 19th book in publisher Boss Fight Books' series of nonfiction titles about game development and gaming culture, and is available in paperback and digital editions. Due to concerns over page count, material on the design of certain bosses was left on the cutting-room floor. I present that material, written from my interviews with the individuals therein and shared with Gamasutra in October 2018, in full below.

**

Mole Knight is one of *Shovel Knight's* most distinctive characters, and not just for his lobster-red armor and stubby legs that flail like an upset crab when players knock him onto his back. Long and flat, his hands extend into red-hot claws that carve through dirt like the proverbial hot knife through butter. "Mole Knight is obsessed with digging," said Yacht Club Games co-founder and *Shovel Knight* director Sean Velasco. "He's obsessed with it; that's all that matters to him, and he's upset with *Shovel Knight* because he wants to be the best at digging."

A second distinctive fixture, more subdued than his claws, is the plume of fire atop Mole Knight's helm. The flame dances even while he stands still, movements that seem trifling but go a long way to cementing the character's identity. "He feels alive. He doesn't seem like just an image," said co-founder and lead artist Nick "Woz" Wozniak. "You can have him sit there and talk to *Shovel Knight,* and he still feels active and alive. That's a thing to consider when you're designing a character: what are its secondary movements? What's the cloth, or scarf, that will trail?"

Woz defined secondary movements as actions that stem from primary movements. Throw a rock into water, and it makes a splash. Secondary movements, ripples extending outward, are the result. Within the context of *Shovel Knight,* a character throws a punch—primary action—and his or her clothing reacts to it.

"When you're designing a character, you want to have interesting parts to their design that have movement that's not directly tied to primary movements, but still enhance them," Woz continued. "That's why a lot of characters will have cloth even though it's not absolutely necessary.

Kratos has a belt that moves around, King Knight has a cape that follows where he goes. That's what makes those characters interesting."

As the programmers on the game, co-founders and *Shovel Knight* programmers David D'Angelo and Ian Flood shared coding duties on bosses. Mole Knight fell under D'Angelo's purview. "It usually begins before there's any programming done," he said of boss design. "Sean and I will likely get together and we'll talk through just basic, 'What could this boss be?'"

Mole Knight is squat, fiery, and armed with claws. Yacht Club suggested slashes, lunges, and a more elaborate sequence where he burrows into a wall and then comes shooting out with claws extended, at which time players could dodge, or hit him with a shovel drop as he flies by. Before Woz got down to the business of animating a character, Velasco sorted through ideas for its attacks and winnowed them down to three or four, the average number of maneuvers used by bosses in NES games. Velasco captured those details in a design document and passed the information on to Woz.

Mole Knight, a boss in Yacht Club Games's *Shovel Knight*.

"At that point some temp or final animations will be given to me, and I'll start figuring out how to piece them together in a way that makes sense," D'Angelo said. "My first step is to put in those attacks almost exactly as they're described, and try to get a feeling for what they're like when they're actually in there."

D'Angelo mulled over the list. Mole Knight revels in speed and chaos. Besides burrowing through and exploding out of walls, he slides along the ground. For versatility, he grows a lava pillar from his fiery plume, pounds the ground to cause a shower of rocks, and creates mounds of debris to trip up players. D'Angelo programmed in those attacks, then played with their implementation and order.

Velasco's design documents described boss moves in rough detail—just enough for Yacht Club co-founder and concept artist Erin Pellon to go on so she could translate his words to illustrations. "Erin would make a few drawings of what it could look like and general shapes," explained Woz. "I would take that and move it into pixel art. I'd take the loose drawing she did and make it into a final form. Then we'll all talk about if it worked or not. If it did, I would model and animate it."

"We wanted the theme of the world, the theme of the character, and the personality of the character to match and be cohesive," Velasco added. "King Knight is arrogant and full of grandeur, but on the inside he's a coward. He lives in a gilded castle and he was planted there by the Enchantress, so it's perfect: everything about him is a facade."

Woz cranked out temporary animations for King Knight's attacks until he arrived at final animations. However, he used these placeholders sparingly. Not only was it easy to get attached to a certain animation and resist changing it, some temp art threw off design. "For Polar Knight, we couldn't use temp animations like we could with King Knight because the size disparity is so huge," Flood said. "You could have King Knight doing all these temp attacks with the idea that we'd put in all these new frames, but if another boss's is three times as large and three times as tall, that completely changes the encounter."

King Knight ended up being one of the easiest bosses to plan and execute. As one of the first bosses players could fight after completing the *Plains of Passage* tutorial zone, he needed to wade in the shallow end of the difficulty pool. "He just plays out all his attacks one by one," said D'Angelo, who programmed the boss, "and it's simple and easy because he's one of the first bosses you see, as opposed to someone like the Enchantress who's extremely built around [progression]."

Baz, one of several wandering bosses players can bump into—or avoid—while traversing *Shovel Knight*'s world map, looks like a cross between the game's Polar Knight boss and one of the Legion of Doom professional wrestlers popular in the WWF during the 1980s.

Unlike Polar Knight, Baz was created by Matt Kowalewski and Woolie Madden, two members of a group of gaming personalities called the Best Friends Zaibatsu, a Japanese term that refers to a conglomerate of businessmen. The best friends adopted the term ironically. While they do indeed run a business, they're a far cry from the image of stern-faced Japanese businessmen wearing suits and clutching briefcases that the term conjures up.

"I think what sets us apart is that we only play the games we're interested in, and not necessarily what's popular," Kowalewski explained. "A lot of our fans can tell what we're enthusiastic about even if it's strange or obscure. While our channel grows pretty slowly, our fanbase sticks around through it all."

Kowalewski and Woolie discovered Baz during an episode of *Fighterpedia*, a show where the duo share facts about fighting games. In the pilot, they mine Capcom's sketches for rejected *Street Fighter II* characters and come across Zubaz, a stereotypical meathead character whose rippling muscles bulge beneath a gym outfit with his name emblazoned on the front. According to the sketch, Zubaz could summon lightning from the sky or crack his whip to deal damage from a distance. "We fell in love with how awful his entire existence was, and thus naturally decided to give him the personality of this unstoppable force to be reckoned with, making a cameo in every single episode," said Woolie.

When the two friends caught wind of the *Shovel Knight* Kickstarter, they talked excitedly of the game's prospects. The game also seemed the stage on which Capcom's rejected concept could make his video game debut. "We had met Yacht Club at E3 2013 long before *Shovel*

Knight had released and hit it off pretty well," said Kowalewski of meeting the Yacht Club co-founders. "When it came down to Kickstarter rewards, Woolie and I put our heads together to get 'The Baz' included as a boss fight. We knew this was his time—nay, his destiny."

Woolie and Kowalewski pledged to *Shovel Knight*'s $1000 Kickstarter level to become Directors for a Day. As co-directors, they would get to collaborate with Yacht Club on the design of a boss or mid-boss character. "Everyone sent us their various inspirations of what they would like the character to be," Flood explained. "From there, we would turn the character into a concept. If everyone was on board with it, we'd turn the character into a full illustration. Then, like any other feature in the game, we would turn that into a sprite."

Over dinner, Kowalewski and Woolie shared their grand plans for Baz. They had already exchanged emails with Yacht Club and given their elevator pitch on how the character should function. At the meet-and-greet, the group swapped stories of their favorite NES games and talked over concept artwork for Baz. "We described his personality, what type of conversation he should have when encountered, broke down each of his moves in the two phases of the fight and how they should look, as well as how his swinging mechanics should work," Woolie said. "The rest of the fine variables like damage, speed, and challenge was all Yacht Club, including that awesome crybaby animation when he loses."

Every so often, Yacht Club's evaluations of a boss's needs led them to bend their own rules for designing *Shovel Knight*.

Secondary characters in NES games had walk cycles consisting of two frames, whereas the main character might have between four to six frames. Several *Shovel Knight* characters pushed that envelope. "I think Specter Knight and *Shovel Knight* stick out as especially not appropriate for the NES [hardware], just because they have so much animation, but people love how Specter Knight looks," reasoned Sean Velasco, co-founder of Yacht Club Games and director on *Shovel Knight*.

A grim reaper-type character who haunts the Lich Yard, Specter Knight oozes dread. Before they battle, Specter Knight taunts his shovel-wielding foe by insinuating that Shield Knight is beyond saving, and reveals that the Enchantress raised him from beyond the grave. This nugget paints him as a possible anti-hero. Players are left to wonder if he is truly evil, or forced to carry out his mistress's bidding (a quandary answered in 2017's Plague of Shadows expansion pack).

"He wasn't tied to the ground," explained co-founder and lead artist Nick "Woz" Wozniak, "so I could do more with how his legs were positioned, and make him more wraith- and reaper-themed."

Specter Knight capitalizes on his ghostly form by gliding through the air and hurling his scythe, which cuts through the air before returning like a boomerang. More than adhering to his grim reaper character, uprooting Specter Knight left Yacht Club co-founder and programmer Ian Flood unencumbered from concerns that pertained to ground-based bosses. "He doesn't care about collision. In fact all of his attacks teleport or completely ignore collision. Fighting him isn't about reacting and sparring with somebody; it's about obeying their patterns and finding vulnerabilities within them. That's great because it's more of a classic NES boss in many ways."

Once players wear down Specter Knight, he turns out the lights. Fortunately, players are prepared to fight in darkness, having just survived stretches of the Lich Yard featuring the gimmick. While screens cloaked in darkness might have proven tricky to navigate at first, players have been growing proficient in controlling their character. By the time they reach Specter Knight, they might feel a second or two of panic when the boss lair goes dark. Then they remember that they've dealt with this before, and their growing mastery over maneuvering *Shovel Knight*—knowing the arc of his jump, how far he stumbles back after getting hit—lights the way.

"Specter Knight was pretty much all special-attack based: I put in this attack, I put in that attack, then I put in the other one," Flood described. "He summons skeletons, and you've fought skeletons. He summons a darkness veil, but you've [overcome] that before. It's surprising because you weren't expecting it, but it's not wholly new."

Gathering feedback from testers, Yacht Club was surprised to learn that players found one particular move difficult to manage. At certain times during the fight, the reaper flings his scythe. The weapon's sprite is nearly as large as that of its wielder, which overwhelmed some testers. Yacht Club responded by slowing down the scythe, although it still covers a wide swath of air, so players still have to pay attention to dodge it. They also gave players plenty of opportunities to comprehend that timing is their best weapon. Because Specter Knight's string of attacks play out in patterns, and because he drifts between the same locations—above or below two platforms on either side of his lair—players can pick up on where to go and when to go there.

"Just looking at the flow of the game, you [take on] Black Knight, then King Knight, then you go to Specter Knight. It's a little bit of a jump [in difficulty]," Flood admitted. "I think that's okay. It's okay to have differences, but I wonder if there's a way to fix it even more than we have already."

Plague Knight, coded by D'Angelo, is the antithesis of Specter Knight. "It's about finding things to find out how much variety you can get out of these three or four moves, just to begin with," D'Angelo said, laying out the process he used to bring Plague Knight to life. "Once all those attacks are in there and I've figured out an amount of variety, I think, 'how can I stitch these together in a way that makes sense?' I would say there are generally a few go-to ways."

One way, popular in the NES era, is by structuring attacks according to patterns. That worked for Specter Knight, but it wouldn't do for Plague Knight. His text waves and shudders on the screen, giving the impression that he is as volatile as the explosive cauldrons of liquid scattered throughout his Explodatorium stage.

Random attacks present another type of implementation, one Yacht Club rejected. Players should be able to calculate a boss's attacks and discern a pattern, if only to a degree. While Plague Knight's attacks seem random, there's a method to the mad foe's movements. "Plague Knight is always jumping to where the player is and trying to throw bombs at the player," D'Angelo explained, "so having him be pattern-based would be weird because he's much more of a reactive, manic [character]. That part is about figuring out how to lay out attacks in an order that's satisfying for the character."

Plague Knight, a boss who received his own spin-off expansion for the main *Shovel Knight* game.

Explosions can harm the player, but they beget a secondary effect. Detonations rip away chunks of the floor to create holes, complicating navigation. Plague Knight occasionally spits out green fireballs that race along floors and walls, and summons cauldrons that trigger larger explosions when struck. Once again, players rely on their growing mastery to succeed. *Shovel Knight* can hit Plague Knight's bombs at him, just like Black Knight's fireballs, and shovel-dropping on his head bounces players up high out of harm's way.

Building bosses does not end at implementation. Like the first draft of a book, they remain incomplete until Yacht Club puts them through round after round of polishing. "You have to fine-tune how a boss works," said Woz. "Hit boxes change, and then we have to change how big a piece of art is. Specter Knight's scythe was one tile larger than it is now, so we had to tone that down."

Propeller Knight, a swashbuckler armed with a rapier and Heli-Helmet, like a razor-sharp beanie forged from a propeller, is one of the last bosses on the road leading to the Tower of Fate. He's slim and nimble, and stands out as one of the most stylish enemies in the game's roster—equal parts debonair and roguish.

Propeller Knight's temperament comes into focus when contrasted against Specter Knight's grim demeanor, Plague Knight's eccentricity, and Polar Knight's stoicism. "Propeller Knight seems like he would be a romantic, dashing sky pirate just by how he looks," said Velasco. "We tried to make his dialogue equally haughty and arrogant, but also fun-loving."

The flighty boss sprang from a purposefully hasty bout of brainstorming between Velasco and Pellon. "We said, 'We're only going to give ourselves ten minutes apiece to draw these things, so we've got to be quick,'" Velasco remembered. They approached the white board, took up markers, and set off. "The initial drawings look very little like what we ended up with, but Propeller Knight of the Flying Machine started with a propeller on his head. He was a cocksure flying ace. That's what seemed intuitive for us."

Propeller Knight stands tall and lanky, a svelte build ideal for a fencing pirate who bounds and soars to throw off his opponent's rhythm. Woz elaborated on his sprightliness when the time came to draw up animations. "His poses are extreme. He's very dramatic in how he positions his arms and where he puts emphasis on the weight of his body. He's almost contorted in his idle animation, and that comes through in many of his poses."

Propeller Knight moves in a blur. His opening salvo consists of blink-and-you'll-miss-them thrusts—right to left across the screen then back again. As the fight progresses, cannonballs fired from galleons flying in the background fall like hail. Despite Propeller Knight's speed and fleet of cannons, players are faster. They need only fight aggressively and use the right attacks at the right time, such as shovel drops to counter lunges. "In some games there are bosses where they'll do a pattern where they'll attack four times, and then during the fifth attack, they're vulnerable and you can get in exactly three hits," Flood said. "I was always happy with the fact that all the boss fights in *Shovel Knight* had a great amount of player choice in them: You can beat them as fast as you want to if you know what you're doing."

One pivotal factor in designing bosses lies in how cinematic a fight should be. *Mega Man* games culminate in a showdown with Dr. Wily, who pilots screen-filling behemoths such as the Guts Dozer. Some giant-sized bosses fade in and out, leaving players to anticipate when and where they will materialize. In their study of NES-style design, Yacht Club deduced that such flair should be used sparingly. Cinematic attacks such as bosses disappearing and reappearing work well provided they pop back into sight quickly, staving off boredom and frustration.

"That's probably the upper limit for how long an enemy can be on-screen and invincible, in terms of what we think would be a good, acceptable flow," D'Angelo said of Dr. Wily's brief disappearing acts. "We let that guide the process when we put in a boss or an encounter. If the boss is there, you should be able to hit him. Everything else is just weaving in your attacks."

Tinker Knight is at once the most diminutive and gargantuan associate of the Order of No Quarter, and along with the Enchantress, one of the two most cinematic.

Yacht Club Games co-founder and programmer David D'Angelo gave Kickstarter backers another inside look at Tinker Knight, mechanical master of Clockwork Tower. "I actually programmed that boss live on Twitch," he said. A streaming service engineered for games, Twitch lets players broadcast themselves playing their favorite titles or watching others play, chatting with viewers as they go along. In planning *Shovel Knight*'s Kickstarter, the team hit on a way to subvert Twitch: Invite backers to watch them design parts of their game, even accepting suggestions.

"It was weird because we didn't have a design for [Tinker Knight], which was pretty unusual for us, going into a boss," D'Angelo continued, reflecting on his live stream. "'Hey, here's Tinker Knight with a wrench, and a big mech. Make a boss out of it.' Okay! I just free-wheeled it on Twitch."

At the end of Clockwork Tower, players drop into a dark room occupied only by a workbench. A tiny man wearing a welding mask and spotless apron looks up and crosses wits against *Shovel Knight*. Tinker Knight flails and trips, wide open for players to unload slashes and shovel drops. Just when players think they've won, the floors give way and players drop into Tinker Knight's second workshop.

"A lot of times," Yacht Club co-founder and *Shovel Knight* director Sean Velasco said, "we joke that, 'Let's do a floor break here.' A floor break is how you up the ante. With Tinker

Knight, we said, 'Oh, yeah, we'll do a floor break.' In the new campaign—n 'Specter of Torment'—every boss floor breaks, just because when you're [making] a side scroller, there are only a few ways you can clear the scene; having the floor break out from underneath you is one of the easiest ways to do it."

Now that he's lured *Shovel Knight* into his trap, Tinker Knight unveils his War Machine, a gigantic tank covered in spikes and missile launchers and armed with a striped lance. Tinker Knight sits behind the wheel of his mechanical monster, shooting off homing missiles and unloading bombs. "The idea was, we want to have this tiny character that kind of sucks at first, but then at the end he gets into this giant [machine] and is all cool and badass," Velasco said. "The War Machine is kind of an homage to the Guts Dozer [in *Mega Man 2*], but we also tried to break off and do our own thing."

Yacht Club felt some apprehension in designing the War Machine. "The second form of Tinker Knight was weird because we'd just come off Double Dragon Neon and we'd done this huge tank battle, and no one liked it," said D'Angelo.

The issue, he explained, was that Double Dragon Neon's tank battle took the form of a platforming challenge in a game centered on simple brawling—a square peg crammed through a round hole. The object was for players to avoid projectiles and climb up the tank to deal damage to a weak spot. "There were bullets all over the screen, and they were hard to see because there were so many," D'Angelo continued. "They were all over the place and it was hard to tell where your goal was. It was a mess. We were doing [Tinker Knight's] tank battle, and everyone was like, 'This is going to be a disaster.' It wasn't like a normal boss; it's a platforming challenge, not a boss fight per se."

Over multiple rounds of play testing, Yacht Club solved the issue that had plagued Double Dragon Neon. In Tinker Knight's second phase, players must mount the tank and bash War Machine's head. To do this, they can pogo off a bouncy bomb and land on the lance, but the lance twirls in mesmerizing fashion, like a barber shop pole, so players must keep their footing to avoid falling off. Another option is to wait for Tinker Knight to fire a line of missiles that come in threes and fly in a stair-step pattern.

"We tried to think about, how is *Shovel Knight* going to get up there?" Velasco said. "We came up with the idea of jumping on missiles. Ever since *Contra III*, I would say that all of us consider jumping and riding on a missile to be a quintessential video game thing: 'We've got to have riding on a missile.'"

Missiles blast out of shoulder-mounted launchers, giving players a hazard to be mindful of when they ascend to War Machine's head. The game lets them inflict only so much damage before the War Machine bucks them off. They knew that figuring out how best to reach the boss's weak spot would be more rewarding than getting lucky once and bringing the battle to a close.

"It felt like a lot," D'Angelo said, "but it was still small and understandable, learning what elements you had to interact with. Each part is a discrete stage. When you're at the bottom, the missiles at the top aren't coming even close to you, so you don't have to think about them at all. All you're thinking about is [climbing] his lance. So it's like, 'Once I figure out that step, then I can think about the next step.' Having none of those intermingling attacks helps with the clarity of [the fight]."

6

Randy Littlejohn
Director of Photography on Gabriel Knight 2

Directing a movie is hardly a one-person job. There are actors to guide, props to gather and/or build, locations to scout and/or build, scenes to block, and postproduction edits to make. That's just the tip of the iceberg. In the era of FMV (full-motion video) games, directing a blockbuster production such as Sierra's *The Beast Within*—aka *Gabriel Knight 2* (GK2)—was an equally momentous task. Bigger, in fact. On top of every consideration that must be accounted for on the set of a Hollywood film, directors who pulled together FMV games had to accumulate dozens upon dozens of hours of extra and vital footage, having to account for every possible action that players choose to take, or *not* take.

Will Binder had years of experience when he took the helm of *The Beast Within*, but he could hardly expect to pull off the whole production on his own. Enter Randy Littlejohn.

Randy was the director of photography on *The Beast Within*, a fancy term for "the person responsible for bringing the director's cinematic vision to life." Every actor, every prop, every mood or theme that had to be conveyed to immerse players in the game's supernatural setting more fully—if it appeared on your screen and responded to the click of your dagger-shaped mouse cursor, Randy played a huge part in putting it there.

Oh, and he also happened to be the guy responsible for getting real, live wolves to snarl at him, all in the name of slaking your thirst for point-and-click entertainment.

I got the chance to talk to talk to Randy about his background in theater, how he got his start at Sierra On-Line, and the details involved in bringing (in)arguably the greatest FMV game ever made to life.

**

Craddock:	The bio on your website describes you as a creative kid with an interest in art and music. Could you talk more about where those interests came from?
Randy Littlejohn:	Who knows where that inclination comes from? But my mother had something to do with it. She was a pretty good artist-musician-composer

and had an interest in theatre in high school. During her childhood in Los Angeles, her best friend's mother was a professional movie extra, so the two of them often found themselves playing amongst the movie and TV sets at the various studios. Mom married and settled down to raise a family, but I think she often wondered what life might have been had she gone into the entertainment business instead. She had big screen looks and was pretty talented, so who knows how that would've turned out?

I showed some interest towards music and art early on, so naturally Mom was right there to nurture me along. On rainy days we'd do ink and watercolor or pastel drawings at the kitchen table together (that's the only time I wasn't outside). When I was in third grade she decided to start me on piano lessons. I wasn't a great student. A few years later she wondered what other instrument I might like to try. I settled on the trumpet and played from grade school through high school. When I was a kid Mom use to direct skits at the Country Club, which inspired me to get my friends together to put on plays in our garage. In high school I picked up guitar and started singing. I wasn't very good, but it was the times. How many people who grew up in the Sixties didn't pick up the guitar?

When I was 16, Mom's childhood best friend, who had become a professional extra like her mother, was working on the TV show *Bonanza* (1959–1973). She offered studio passes for me and a friend if I wanted to come down and look around. So a buddy of mine with a '55 Chevy and I left Santa Maria where I grew up and about three hours later showed up at the Paramount Studios gate. The passes, which were signed by Lorne Greene who played Ben Cartwright, immediately got us into the studio. To our great surprise, there was no one waiting for us, so we wondered around the exterior standing sets for hours, amazed that no one wondered what the heck a couple of high school kids were doing there. It was great fun.

Tired of that, we started poking around soundstages and found an unlocked door. It was the soundstage where they had the exterior and interior sets for the Cartwright house. We snuck in and the place was busy. The cast and crew were shooting an episode. Somehow, no one paid any attention to us. We watched them shoot a couple of scenes and then snuck back out. It all made a big impression on me.

A year later I tried out for a part in a HS play and became the voice of God in the play "JB." Not long after that I got the part of the character File in "The Rainmaker."

I took a little time off for a stint in the Coast Guard, but by the time I got out I was ready to pursue the arts in college.

Craddock: How did you discover computers? How did computers influence your love of creative expression?

Randy Littlejohn: I took an experimental psychology class in the early '70s. As part of that class we had to use punch cards to get a computer to do a simple pie chart. If you made one little mistake in the card stack, you had to start all over again. I was not impressed.

When I got out of college, my first real job was producer-director at a small television station. I wrote, produced, lit, directed, shot, edited, and voiced 30 second commercials. It was great fun because I had the chance to get my hands on every part of the process. While I was working at the station we went from analogue effects to digital video effects. That was my first exposure to computers that you could do cool creative stuff with, so I immediately changed my mind about the worth of computers.

Not long after that my father gave me an I-99/4A home computer. With it was a text adventure game: *Pirate Cove* written by Scott Adams. That's when it became clear to me that personal computers had potential as a storytelling platform.

Craddock:	What was your experience with video and computer games prior to joining the industry? Did you play much in your free time?
Randy Littlejohn:	When I landed my job at Sierra On-Line, I'd played an early arcade racing game, a lot of *Space Invaders* and *Pac-Man*, and one text adventure game: *Pirate Cove*.
Craddock:	What field or fields of study did you pursue in college?
Randy Littlejohn:	My first major was music. I soon realized that I wasn't serious enough about it to succeed. I took a lot of psychology classes. I studied theatre and excelled there, but the allure of film and TV production pulled me in that direction. I graduated with a BA in Speech and Drama, but with a lot of credits in film and TV production classes.
Craddock:	Did you have your eye on any particular line of work after college, or were you still cultivating numerous creative skills?
Randy Littlejohn:	By the time I ran out of money and was therefore forced to end my career as a student, I knew that I wanted to be in film or television production. I didn't have much time to stress over it, because soon after I left my graduate studies behind, I got that job as a television producer-director.
Craddock:	What jobs did you perform prior to entering the games industry?
Randy Littlejohn:	I was a television producer-director for five years and then produced infomercials for a year. It was a fun gig. I sold everything from miniature steam powered engines, to robotic vacuum cleaners dressed up as house pets, to glow in the dark underwear. That company went through hard times and I suddenly found myself jobless.
	For a while I worked in a used and antiquarian bookstore and then sold used cars briefly. I loathed selling used cars, but there was that night when another salesman and I took a Vette and a Porsche out to see which was faster… It was four months after I started that job that I got a call that I'd landed the Sierra job. On my birthday. Nice present.
Craddock:	Sierra was the first games company you worked for, correct? How'd you get the opportunity to interview there?

Randy Littlejohn: Yes. My parents lived in Mariposa in the Nineties. I'd been away from them for a long time, so I moved there after I left the infomercial gig. The bookstore I mentioned earlier was in Oakhurst, not far from Mariposa. While at the bookstore, I discovered that Sierra was building a blue-screen facility at their Oakhurst studio in preparation for a live-action adventure game. I started calling them. I was relentless. And had something to offer.

Phantasmagoria.

Craddock: What made you decide to work in the games business as opposed to, say, movies, television, or theater?

Randy Littlejohn: There's the plan and then there's what happens. It wasn't as if I decided on one over the other. It was simply a confluence of interest, opportunity, and qualifications.

Craddock: What was your first project at Sierra?

Randy Littlejohn: I was the Lighting-Camera person on *Phantasmagoria*, working under a DP. I also helped with editing cutscenes.

Craddock: How far along was Sierra's Oakhurst-based, blue-screen studio when you joined?

Randy Littlejohn: When I started at Sierra they hadn't started building the studio yet. I worked with two other people in the old video production facility until the new space (in one half of the Oakhurst water company building) was ready. The three of us and Bill Crow built the blue-screen studio under Bill's direction. Bill was the studio head and quite an engineer.

                         There was a large space for the blue-screen cove on the ground floor. Immediately adjoining, there was an area for construction and storage. The ground floor also included a kitchen, a greenroom, three (if I remember correctly, but don't hold me to it) dressing rooms, and a restroom. Upstairs was the control room with big windows that looked out over the blue-screen area. On the ground floor there was a large pair of doors leading out of the blue-screen area to a parking lot, which came in handy for bring in props, furniture, and such.

During the shoot for *Phantasmagoria* we were all learning. We didn't have the lights we needed to do more than get proper exposures—nothing artful. The blue-screen area was not large enough to keep blue reflection off of the actors, which causes technical issues, without resorting to heroic measures. The lighting grid wasn't quite high enough to get proper lighting angles. The air conditioning system was noisy, so we had to shut it off for sound takes, but then it'd get hot in the studio.

The facility wasn't a proper sound stage, so we also had to stop and wait for planes to fly over before continuing with a sound take. The blue-screen walls were built facing each other (rather than off-angle), which caused echo problems when trying to record clean audio. The gear in the control room all worked well, despite the fact that we were still putting the final touches on the control room when we went into production. Kudos to Bill Crow.

Bottom line, we had the bare essentials needed to pull off *Phantasmagoria*, but there were issues we had to work around. We were far more ready for GK2, and it shows.

Craddock: What anecdotes from *Phantasmagoria*'s production can you share with us?

Randy Littlejohn: Because I had a background in video and film production, I could see right away that while there was a game design document, pre-production for the FMV elements had not been properly considered. I spoke up, but it was like so much smoke in the wind. Consequently, each day the production crew and the actors did a lot of standing around, somewhere between bemused and embarrassed, whilst people above our pay grade argued about what to do next. A lot of money was wasted. Had pre-production been done properly, each minute of each production day would have been thoroughly mapped out. Pre-production is inexpensive. Production is expensive. It makes sense to put time into pre-production to make it possible to efficiently use expensive production time.

I believe that *Phantasmagoria* was the first FMV video game to use a computer controlled camera motion system. How it works: the physical camera motion is controlled by servo motors directed by code. That same code could be used to create the motion of the virtual camera capturing the computer generated background animation. This maintains all the correct relationships between the live-action camera angles, subjects, and virtual backgrounds. The end effect is as if the entire composite was captured by a single camera. We had a crew with the computer controlled camera system come in for a day to cover a major scene. A very cool day.

Right before the first production day, I went to a little get together for cast and crew at one of the a-frame cabins around Bass Lake, not far from the Oakhurst studio. The place was full of people I didn't know. I got a beer and sat in a couch. Movement caught my eye and I turned to look. Victoria Morsell was coming in from a little balcony outside wearing some gossamer thing and backlit by the sun. The rest of the world faded away. It was like a movie entrance. That moment is indelible in my mind. Beautiful woman.

Craddock: What were some of the big and small ways that shooting an FMV game differed from shooting non-interactive cinema?

Randy Littlejohn: The major difference, of course, is the extra coverage needed for player choices. In a film or TV show the audience sees an efficient series of shots that tell a story. If it's not essential, it isn't there. In *Phantasmagoria*, the player discovered the story elements in a roundabout way, exploring much more material than would be shot for linear storytelling. An average feature film is 90–120 pages of script. The script for GK2 was something like 600 pages—the equivalent of five feature films.

In addition, the player controlled the motion of Adrienne—a live-action character. The player could turn her left or right, walk right or left, or turn around and walk back. All of that had to be shot. We put Victoria in the middle of the blue-screen area on a grid and had her stand in a neutral position. The camera was locked down. We taped her turning right, and then back to her neutral position. We did the same thing for every direction she could turn to without being awkward, with a return to the same neutral position after each movement. Then we taped her turning to the left and taking a few walking steps. We did that for all directions too.

We also taped "fidgets". These were designed to keep Adrienne looking "alive" while she wasn't being moved. Victoria started in her neutral position, and then did something like brushing hair from her face, or a big sigh, or just any little natural movement, and then back to her neutral position. We did several of these for variety. By putting each of these movements in a database, all starting and ending at a neutral position, code could call each up seamlessly as needed in real time as the player steered their avatar around the sets.

Craddock: How did your work on *Phantasmagoria* lead to the opportunity to work on *The Beast Within*: A Gabriel Knight Mystery?

Randy Littlejohn: As production proceeded on *Phantasmagoria*, I quickly ended up doing all of the lighting and camera work. Once the DP contractor saw that I knew what I was doing, he just stood aside and let me go for it. GK2 was scheduled to start production pretty much the moment we wrapped Phantaz. I lobbied for the DP job and got it based on my Phantaz work and background.

Craddock: What was your specific role on GK2?

Randy Littlejohn: Director of photography.

Craddock: Before we get into nitty-gritty, could you give an overview of your collaboration with other managers on the production? Will Binder and Darlou Gams, the art designer, for example?

Randy Littlejohn:	The blue-screen facility was on the other side of town from the studio main building. During the two FMV productions I rarely went into the main building. There just wasn't time. The FMV crew was pulling 12–14 hour days six days a week. So every day I interacted with director Will Binder, assistant director Gil Neuman, production manager David Plaskett, studio head Bill Crow, two production assistants, and an engineer in the control room. Other than makeup people, costumers, and actors, I rarely saw anyone else, which was okay. As DP, there was no need to interact with anyone else.
Craddock:	Besides experience in lighting, you brought a wealth of other creative abilities on set with you. Did you get the opportunity to use them during GK2's production?
Randy Littlejohn:	It's kind of you to say so, but I was up to my ears in camera setups, lighting, and trying to figure out how to effectively wrap actors into a pre-shot background image. I had time for little else. I did, however, help out with editing cutscenes, and early on I created a Microsoft Access database to help organize pre-production. You could call up a scene number and list all of the actors, props, costumes, and setups needed. It's how we produced the daily call sheets too.
Craddock:	How were Ludwig's famous castles reconstructed in the game? What sorts of details did you need to make them look as true to life as possible?
Randy Littlejohn:	Every setup started with an analysis of the background plates shot in Europe. Where are we? What is the nature of the light on the scene? How high or low was the camera that took the background image (plate)? Was the background plate camera tilted up or down or was it shooting from the side? What focal length was used? I asked for that information to be recorded so that we could replicate it with the studio camera. I only got some of this information, so often it was process of eyeballing and adjustments. If we didn't try to replicate the circumstances of the background plate camera, the live-action elements would look off when composted with the plate.

If the background plate is an interior, what props and furniture do we need to bring into the studio for the actors to interact with? Furniture and props were brought up from a place that services film and TV production in Los Angeles. What were the sources of light? What was the nature and color of the light? *Et cetera.*

Sometimes we tried to make the background plate "3D" by matching blue-screen-painted foamcore or a blue-screen-painted apple boxes or flats to elements in the background plate so that an actor would appear to walk in back of or sit on an element in the plate. I often used a big monitor in the blue-screen area with a half-dissolve between the background plate and the studio camera as an aid in lining things up. It also gave the actors an idea of the environment their characters were in.

In one shot, Grace wakes up from a dream in Gabe's castle. Joanne Takahashi (Grace) was in a real bed. In the background plate, a full moon shines through windows. I tried to light Joanne softly from the camera side with just enough exposure to capture detail. The light was filtered to simulate a cool nighttime light. I edge-lit her with bright, white specular light from as close as I could get to the angle of the moon shining through the background plate behind her. The final composite appears to be grace in a darkened room with moonlight shining on her.

Occasionally, we needed to build flats to replicate something in the background plate we wanted the actors to interact with, such as the front door of Gabriel's castle.

Craddock: Let's talk about specific scenes. The intro to Chapter 1 did a great job setting the scene: Gabriel is struggling with his latest novel, and a mob of villagers sporting flashlights ("Shouldn't those be torches?") arrives at his door to request help solving a murder believed to have been committed by a werewolf. You posted a photograph from this scene on your website. Could you describe the equipment and props seen in the picture, and how they came together to create the cinematic players watched when they got their hands on the game?

Randy Littlejohn: I took this shot from a catwalk outside the control room. That's why I'm not standing by the camera. In this setup, we needed the actors to be able to interact with the front door to the castle, so we built a flat with a door to replicate the doorway in the location plate.

Dave Plaskett can be seen standing in front of the camera with headphones on. Gill Neuman is standing to the right of the crowd at the door in a white shirt. Around the periphery of the setup are sound blankets hung on c-stands to soak up the audio brightness and echo of the bluescreen cove.

I don't remember for sure, but the camera might have been a Sony Betacam SP BVW-D600P. It's sitting on a Vinten tripod with a fluid head. There's a c-stand holding a flag over the camera to eliminate lens flairs. You can see a boom hanging over the scene with a mike at the end for capturing dialogue.

I lit most everything with Fresnel instruments of various sizes and Chimera soft boxes, like the one just to the left of the camera. The light in the foreground to the right is a Fresnel, which is a focusable instrument that gets its name from French physicist Augustin-Jean Fresnel, who originally invented this instruments lens type for lighthouses. The blue screen was lit from the lighting grid above and from instruments on the floor, the idea being to light it as evenly as possible.

To keep blue reflection off of the actors (which can cause technical issues), I moved them as far away from the blue screen as possible. To control light on the actors I often lit them from the floor, rather than using lights on the grid above, but not always. I had a lot more instruments to play with during GK2 production than when we shot Phantaz [*Phantasmagoria*], which gave me a lot of flexibility.

The lights you see have various jobs from simple illumination to causing effects to match the lighting in the background plate.

In the lower right hand corner is a table that held monitors and equipment for analyzing the light on the scene. I needed to make sure that highlights, shadows, and blacks were with our technical specifications. The equipment helped me keep the highlights from blowing out and losing detail and to make sure that I was capturing usable detail in the shadows. I pushed the envelope, trying to use every possible bit of latitude the Beta SP format and studio camera would allow.

The ideal outcome was a seamless composite of live-action elements wrapped into the background plate.

Craddock: What challenges did GK2's location shoots pose?

Randy Littlejohn: There are always little challenges, but that's part of the fun. Almost everything we shot was blue screen, so I looked forward to discovering that a real world with a real sun existed somewhere beyond the studio walls. If memory serves, there were just three location shoots. We shot a dream sequence in the snow up in the mountains above Oakhurst, shot at a ranch out in the Central Valley to capture what would become Ludwig's carriage, and shot in a barn outside of Coarsegold.

For the snow shoot we had to make sure that Joanne Takahashi [Grace] didn't break a leg as she ran past the camera or end up with hypothermia. At the barn we had limited access to electricity, so I had to be frugal with lighting. We were shooting day for night, which was a little problematic, since outside light had many ways to sneak in and had to be controlled. We shot with a very talkative horse in the background, so we had to work around that. I think the horse vocalized at the end of the take we put in the game and Dean played off of that without missing a beat.

Craddock: Conversely, was there a particular location where you enjoyed filming due to it being more conducive to getting work done smoothly?

Randy Littlejohn: The fact that no matter how well prepared one is, stuff happens. Whether or not work gets done smoothly is all about preparation. All of our locations were scouted ahead of time and served their purposes very well.

Craddock: What was involved in shooting outdoor scenes set at night, such as Gabriel and von Glower hunting the werewolf near the hunting lodge?

Randy Littlejohn: The scene you're referring to was shot inside the blue-screen facility. The background plates were of a forest night. My lighting had to match that. I used an instrument that projects a pattern to simulate moonlight filtering through branches and leaves and used cool filters to match the color in the background plates. The bushes and branches Gabriel has to come through were hastily harvested from right outside the studio, brought in, and tied to c-stands so that they stuck into the frame from the sides. Smoke and mirrors.

Craddock: So many scenes took place at the opera house in the final chapter of the game. Jane Jensen told me that some filming took place at an actual opera house. How much of the scenes in the game's opera house were filmed live versus via blue screen?

Randy Littlejohn: All of the stuff for the opera house was shot in Seattle by a different crew. I wasn't involved. We may have shot some stuff connected to those scenes in the studio as well. I don't remember.

Craddock: As the director of photography, what was your goal in preparing for a scene? What elements did you need to keep in mind, and how do you go about capturing those elements?

Randy Littlejohn: The goal was always to seamlessly wrap the live-action elements into the background plate. So it became a matter of analyzing the background plate for original camera position, height, angle, lens used, etc. and for the nature, source(s) and color of the light on the scene. Then my job was to consider what I had to work with in terms of lighting instruments, props, furniture, and tricks of the trade to create live-action elements that could be composited into the background plate and look completely natural. What would best be lit from the lighting grid? What would best be lit from light stands on the studio floor? What instruments would give me the effect I was looking for? How could I make it look as interesting and 3D as possible?

   Beyond that, it was my job to make the actors look good. I often used soft boxes for both fill and key light. That means that the general light used for proper exposure, plus the light made to look like the primary light source, was all coming from soft boxes. This created a soft, flattering, and romantic quality of light. I edge-lit and backlit with more specular light from Fresnels to add attractive highlights and to separate the actors from the background to make the scene more 3D. In dramatically edgy scenes, I used all Fresnels for a more specular, gritty look.

The Beast Within: A Gabriel Knight Story, aka Gabriel Knight 2.

Craddock: How much of the Oakhurst studio did you have to work with? Did you find yourself having to tear down scenes and prep for new ones hastily, or was the crew able to spread out a little?

Randy Littlejohn: We didn't have the space or available crew to have folks working on the next setup while we were shooting the preceding one on the day's schedule. On GK2, it was just me and one or two assistants doing the setups, with Bill and an engineer above in the control room, plus a contract audio guy coming in to set up audio when we had the shot ready. Because of the tight schedule, we had to do our setups as quickly as possible and go. As soon as we got the shot, it was time to hastily break everything down and start on the next setup. Since we did most of the shooting on the blue-screen stage, with all our gear gathered around us, we could really move. If we'd been shooting at various locations, we couldn't have kept up with the schedule without hiring more crew.

Craddock: What were some of the most difficult blue-screen scenes to shoot?

Randy Littlejohn: Sometimes the background plates demanded the camera to be farther away from the actors than was possible within the confines of the studio, so I had to improvise.

One time the camera was supposed to be far above the characters below. The ceiling of the studio was only two stories high, and was covered by the lighting grid. I put the camera on the top of a rolling ladder and placed it between lights on the lighting grid for a little more height and pointed it straight down towards the actors below using a special mount. I faked the extra distance by using an extremely wide lens.

Another time I had to put the studio camera in the adjoining construction area and shoot across the blue-screen cove to the opposite corner to get the camera far enough away from the actors to match the background plate.

There's a scene where Grace walks across a bridge towards the front door of Gabriel's castle. That was another time I had to place the camera in the construction and storage room to make enough room for Joanne to cover the distance needed to match the background plate. Of course, then I had to figure out how to evenly light her entire path so that she wasn't moving in and out of light, since shadows weren't indicated in the background plate.

One time we had to fake an exterior shot of Ludwig in his coach sitting on a village street. The background plate was a composite of a village street and the coach we shot at a ranch in the Central Valley. Our job was to somehow put the actor playing Ludwig into the coach and the actors playing the driver and assistant on the seat at the front of the coach. We sat the Ludwig actor on blue apple boxes and lined up a large piece of blue foamcore with the coach window to partially obscure him, as was called for by the angle of the camera that shot the coach.

I controlled the light falling on him to indicate that he was inside the coach. I used a shadow caused by the foamcore, which worked perfectly. We built a platform of blue apple boxes and boards for the other two actors to sit on, carefully matching edges with the coach in the background plate. The finished composite was pretty convincing.

Craddock: What are some factors that can cause a scene to become more or less difficult to film than expected? (i.e., actors needing more direction)

Randy Littlejohn: As the person responsible for capturing the images (not someone worried about performances), the main gotcha that cropped up was being presented with a background plate that I'd never seen before, which seemingly called for something that would be impossible within the confines of the blue-screen cove. We really had to think on our feet a few times. There are always little things that come up, but that's normal for film and video production. Stuff happens. The job is to know your stuff so that quick adjustments can be made.

I will add that our GK2 actors were pros, capable, and prepared for their scenes. Will worked with them while we were setting up. We seldom did more than a couple of takes.

Craddock: Could you describe a typical (or perhaps an atypical) day during the three-month production? How many responsibilities were you juggling, and how'd you manage them?

Randy Littlejohn: I'd drive down to Oakhurst from Bass Lake Heights where I lived at the time early in the morning and meet the team at the production studio. We get the control room up and running, get the studio camera going, drink some coffee and pow wow about the plan for the day and begin working on the first setup. Will and the actors would show up a bit later. We'd work like crazed worker bees until lunch. Often times cast and crew would go off to eat somewhere together. Lunches were great fun. We all come back and work like crazed worker bees until long after the sun went down. After the actors left for the day, for they were protected by SAG rules, the studio crew would stay and get some other things done, like editing cutscenes. Twelve to fourteen hours after we first showed up in the morning, we'd head for home—or the occasional party, or poker, or in my case the gym.

I was responsible for camera setup, lighting, and for coming up with novel ways to make the actors, set pieces, etc. wrap nicely into the background image. Every day offered different challenges. It was a great experience. There were tense times, but the work was very, very satisfying.

One time we had part of a day set aside for wolves. On that day a trainer showed up with four or five trained wolves. He set up an invisible electric barrier that the wolves understood to stay within. My job was to get the best shots of them I could. At one point I had the camera mounted on a hi hat, a mount for setting up the camera very near the floor. I was lying on my stomach shooting up at the wolves, who happened to be pretty interested in what I was doing. We were separated by just a few feet at one point. It was very cool to be so close to wolves. There was another time we needed a wolf to snarl. That was exciting.

Another time a car was brought into the blue-screen cove. We needed to composite it and Dean with an exterior background plate. The challenge was that cars are shiny. Since it was supposed to be outside, there could be only one apparent source of light—the sun. Of course, the car was under a lighting grid with numerous lights fired up to light the blue screen. So it was a real pain trying to make sure it didn't look like it was sitting on a planet with multiple suns. Plus, the blue-screen cove reflected across the surfaces of the car, which made for technical issues. It was a matter of using dulling spray, getting the car as far away from the blue-screen cove as possible, using large silks to break up reflections from individual lights and the use of a powerful magical spell.

One day we had a tiger paw bathtub on the set complete with sudsy water and a semi-naked actor. The problem was that the water reflected the blue screen, and that caused technical issues. We thought we'd solved the problem by making more bubbles, but the bubbles were reflecting the blue screen too. We moved the tub as far from the blue-screen cove as possible, used some flags, and once again invoked a powerful magical spell.

Craddock: What was the process of editing a scene in post? What were you looking for? What elements needed to be added?

Randy Littlejohn: It was a matter of calling up all of the background plates for a scene, cuing up the video tape for each shot in the scene, and then trying to get a good, clean composite for each setup. Once we had the raw footage composited with the background images, we did a color pass to make sure that all of the shots looked like they belonged together. Once we had all of the composited and color balanced shots for the scene, we began constructing the scene for good flow and timing. Once a scene was edited, it was digitized, compressed, and sent off to the art department where the scene files were further processed to achieve a certain look.

Craddock: Did elements sometimes need to be scrubbed out, either because they were of poor quality, or broke continuity?

Randy Littlejohn: During GK2, all of the scenes were planned out ahead of time. We knew which shots we needed, and that's all we shot. We couldn't just come up with stuff, because the background images we had to match were pre-shot. They predetermined what setups we had to shoot, so we didn't end up with problems like that. I'm not sure how much the art department changed the files in post.

Craddock: What scene stands out as your favorite? (You can cheat and choose more than one if you like.)

Randy Littlejohn: From the point of view of a DP, I guess it would be the scene with Dean (Gabriel), Peter Lucas (Baron Friedrich von Glower), Melanie Good (Detta), and Dave Plaskett (Günther). In the scene, Gabriel is loosening up, enjoying himself after a good deal of wine with Von Glower in his house, when suddenly a female friend of Von Glower shows up, Detta. She's quickly all over Von Glower and Gabe offers to leave, but Von Glower says nonsense. He whispers into Detta's ear, and before Gabriel knows what hit him, she's on his lap. Soon she leads him off to a bedroom.

I like the scene because it was a complex setup and had a little of everything—good actors, good dialogue, furniture on the set, and props. Von Glower's living room is sunken, so there are stairs that come down into it from a hallway above that leads to the front door. Of course, the stairs were only in the background plate, so we had to build the stairs with blue boxes and match their height to the top edges of the stairs in the background plate. The hallway at the top of the stairs had to be faked with a blue platform the actors could walk on. At the top of the stairs, there was a wall. Of course the wall was only in the background plate, but the actors had to make entrances from in back of that wall, so it was necessary to match the edge of the wall with a blue flat that the actors could make their entrances from behind.

The blue elements had to be lit well so that they would disappear into the background plate without difficulty. On the other hand, I needed to make the rest of the lighting appropriate for a comfortable living room scene. It was a nice challenge and a lot of fun to set up. It turned out pretty well.

I also liked the bedroom scenes, first with Detta and Gabe, then with Von Glower and Gabe. In the background plate, the bedroom was lit by light coming in from a door that opened to a lit hallway. I wanted to light for a night scene in the bedroom and get the feeling of light coming in from the hallway, providing the only illumination. I also wanted people entering or exiting the bedroom into the hallway to become silhouettes. Mission accomplished.

Craddock: If you had to pick a favorite project between Phantasmagoria and *Gabriel Knight 2*, which would you choose?

Randy Littlejohn: *Gabriel Knight 2*, easily. The story was great. Setups were much more complex than in Phantaz. Good preproduction made for a fairly efficient shoot. I had more lights to play with, which meant I could set up some artful lighting. There were lots of cool actors, all very nice people. It was a very friendly set. (Thanks, Will). We were overworked, tired, and crazed, but it was a ton of fun and very satisfying.

7

Will Binder
Director on Gabriel Knight 2

Some eras of video game history are more *infamous* than others. In the early 1990s, developers such as Roberta Williams, *King's Quest* creator and "the queen of adventure gaming," and *Gabriel Knight* creator Jane Jensen dreamed of merging Hollywood and video game technology. Games had long been compared to films, and in the '90s, developers got their hands on the technology to make their dream a reality.

That technology was full-motion video (FMV), a way to show scenes in games with actors, sets, props, and green screens instead of sequences of animated pixels and polygons. Results were mixed, to put it lightly. FMV-based games tended to be cheesy, featuring B-list actors and grainy video that struggled on the subpar computer hardware of the day.

Still, there were diamonds in the rough. *The Beast Within*: A *Gabriel Knight* Mystery is arguably the only diamond in the very, very rough period of FMV games. More popularly known as *Gabriel Knight 2*, or just GK2, the game had a solid cast, high production values, and a great script penned by Jane Jensen. GK2 also benefitted from the expertise of Will Binder, who brought Hollywood experience to the production.

**

Craddock: When did you take an interest in movies and visual storytelling, and what influenced that interest?

Will Binder: I loved stories and storytelling as a kid. And of course I loved the movies and television. I guess I started telling stories to myself, like most kids, when I daydreamed. In any given situation, my mind has always seemed to ask the question, "What if this or that happened…." I still do it today. I also loved to draw comics as a kid so it kind of all came together in high school when I started to think about what type of job I'd like to do. I loved drawing and painting and I also loved movies and eventually decided to go to film school to be a director.

As for influences, all of the movies and television that I watched as a kid influenced my interest in making movies as did the directors that I read about. It seemed like an exciting and fun thing to do.

Craddock: Did you want to work in film specifically, or did you eye other creative outlets for storytelling?

Will Binder: I've always loved to draw and paint. It's been a lifelong battle between my need to collaborate with people; making movies verses working alone in a more reflective way as a painter. I love the immediacy of painting, working with my hands, the paint surface, the color, really everything about it. And I also love the dynamics of working with other people and storytelling. I still struggle with it today.

Craddock: Did you attend film school before or after your first job as post-production assistant on *Scent of a Woman*?

Will Binder: I graduated from UCLA film school and then I worked as a post-production assistant (editing) on *Scent of a Woman*, and after that I worked as a production (filming) assistant on *Greedy*.

Craddock: "Film school" conjures up a vague image of lots of cameras and people shouting "Action!" Could you tell us what your journey through film school entailed? What sorts of classes were required? Which were your favorites, and which were most challenging?

Will Binder: I really enjoyed film school, it was great time; everything about it: being a young person, meeting and experimenting creatively with other people who had similar interests. As an undergrad film major, I had to take all kinds of classes including writing classes, film theory, all of the film and video production from directing to camera, sound, editing, etc. It was a really well-rounded curriculum. I would say my favorites were the production and editing classes because we were making movies that people were going to see.

The most challenging aspect was trying to find the money to make our films. Back then we were shooting and editing with celluloid film, not digital video, so it was a lot more expensive.

Craddock: How did you get the job of post-production assistant on *Scent of a Woman*?

Will Binder: I got the assistant job on *Scent* through my good friend Tom Prince, who was an executive at Universal at the time.

Craddock: What exactly does "post-production" entail?

Will Binder: Post-production is everything that happens to the footage after it's shot; the editing, sound, color work, visual effects, etc.

Craddock: What anecdotes from that job can you share?

Will Binder: One time when Al Pacino came to our editing facility in Santa Monica to meet with Martin Brest, the director. Al was very nice, he's an actor's actor, a real artist. He was wearing a bandana on his head and had his dog with him. He said hello to the editing crew and then he and Marty went outside and sat down on the grass divider in the middle of Olympic Blvd. They must have sat there and spoke for an hour while traffic passed them on both sides. I just thought it strange place to have a meeting. And I doubt anybody knew that the guy with the bandana was Al Pacino.

Craddock: What essential skills did you learn from that job?

Will Binder: I would say the biggest thing I learned was how post-production on a large production works. It's a lot different from what I was used to on independent films where you're working with a small crew and everyone wears several hats. Also just being around the A list editors such as William Steinkamp, Michael Tronick, and Harvey Rosenstock. It was a great learning experience, just seeing them in action.

       I got the job on *Greedy* from my friend Tom Prince as well.

Craddock: What did the position of "set assistant" involve?

Will Binder: As one of several production assistants on *Greedy* we worked directly under assistant directors handling everything from getting the actors in and out of hair and make-up, wrangling the extras, standing in for actors, pulling cable for the camera or sound department, clearing the set, noise and crowd control, making copies, getting coffee, dropping off or picking up film, props; whatever was needed. It was hard work and didn't pay a lot, but it was great experience.

Craddock: Which brings us to Sierra. How did you get the job of director on *Gabriel Knight 2*?

Will Binder: I was offered the job to direct by Jane [Jensen] and our producer Sabina Duvall. Joanne Takahashi, [who played Grace [Nakamura], and a couple other actors were the only ones cast and the script wasn't broken down so I was really starting from scratch. Dave Plaskett, the production manager, and I hired Gil Neuman as the first assistant director, and we got to work. At that point we were way behind schedule so we rushed to cast and complete pre-production and then started shooting.

Craddock: What dos breaking down a script entail?

Will Binder: Breaking down a script involves going through each scene to find all of the elements needed in each scene. Elements like: locations, actors, props, etc. After we go through the breakdown process for the entire script, we're able to see which scenes need which elements, and we can begin to create a shooting schedule that saves time and money.

Craddock: What was your level of familiarity with video/computer games prior to getting the job?

Will Binder: I had very little familiarity with video/computer games prior to getting the job.

Craddock: FMV-based games were a new thing around the time of your audition, and thus unproven. What were your thoughts on directing for a video game as opposed to a movie or TV show?

Will Binder: I thought it was a great opportunity and loved the fact that we were working on something that was on the cutting edge. Overall the approach required in directing a game and directing a film are very similar. You work with your actors and your crew to tell a story with images and sound.

       One difference between directing a game and a film is that in a game, the director has to be aware of all the different scenarios that may or may not have happened to a specific character because the story or characters can go in many different directions depending on the choices the player makes. On GK2, for example, something may or may not have happened earlier in Gabriel's adventures depending on the choices the player made, making it difficult for the actor to know exactly what he's been through or where he's at in the story. Because of this, it was tricky at times dealing with the actors and explaining their motivations, state of mind, etc.

Another noticeable difference was some of the specific requirements unique to directing a game. For instance, in many of the scenes in GK2, the actors needed to start and end each scene on a specific mark and in a specific position with a specific expression for continuity purposes because we did not know the next choice the player would make. Also, there were many technical considerations and limitations. *The Beast Within* was basically a giant special effects movie. Ninety percent of the nearly 600 page script was shot on a blue stage. Because of space and monetary reasons we ended up constructing many blue props, fake doors, etc.

This took time and made the lighting more complicated for [photography director] Randy Littlejohn and the crew. And also for Bill Crow and the guys upstairs making sure what we were getting was needed to work with the blue-screen technology. And, because we didn't have motion-control and couldn't move the camera during a shot, we had to take extra care when composing and blocking our shots. Not to mention that our limited budget gave us very little rehearsal time for the cast or crew, making the production even more challenging and rewarding.

Craddock: Besides the obvious perk of a paycheck, what was it about the GK2 project that appealed to you?

Gabriel conversing with a character in *Gabriel Knight 2*.

Will Binder:	There were a lot of things about Jane's story that appealed to me, starting with the theme dealing with the primal duality of man, between human domestication and savagery. I enjoyed the characters, the plot and I loved the way that Jane weaved a believable and compelling story with the Gabriel knight character through actual history. Jane is really an amazing game designer and writer.
Craddock:	What was the process of reading through Jane Jensen's script and deciding how to bring the story to life?
Will Binder:	It was just a matter of understanding the emotional dynamics of the story and deciding how to best capture those dynamics through the choices and execution of what we filmed as well as the direction and feedback given to the actors in any given scene.
Craddock:	What was the back-and-forth between you and Jane Jensen? How much creative control did you have?
Will Binder:	Jane and I worked well together. Once the script was locked and the actors were cast, I didn't change much. Although, in Jane's original script, the opera was mentioned but it was not going to be seen, mainly for financial reasons if remember correctly. Seeing the climactic opera was a pay-off that Dave Plaskett and I thought was vitally important to show. Jane agreed and she added it into the script. Other than that, Jane and I would sometimes speak about motivations or time lines but for the most part, as the director, it was up to me to board, block, and shoot the scenes and direct the actors.
Craddock:	What other directors were involved in the game? Was there a lighting director, for example?
Will Binder:	The production of GK2 was similar to most film or television productions; as the director, I oversaw all aspects of the filming process and was lucky enough to have many talented people working with me. Dave Plaskett was the Production Manager; Gil Neuman was the Assistant Director; Randy Littlejohn was the director of photography who was also was in charge of the lighting; Nathan Gams was the Art Director and so on.
Craddock:	What was the process of collaboration between all the directors? Did they have their purview that you expected them to handle when the time came to film?
Will Binder:	Yes, as the director, I would communicate with the crew continually. Production is a very collaborative process and it's important for everyone to be on the same page. For example, before we filmed a specific scene, I would go over all of the details of that scene, including the blocking with the crew. I worked especially close with my director of photography, Randy Littlejohn, because he was responsible for getting the shot that we wanted. We would usually start by setting a fairly wide master shot of the entire scene. Then we'd start with the coverage, setting up different angles of the same scene to be filmed. We didn't always shoot the entire scene from each angle, but we usually shot some coverage.
Craddock:	Were you involved in casting the actors?
Will Binder:	Yes, I was involved along with Jane Jensen and our producer Sabine Duvall. The only actors that were cast before I took over as the director were Joanne Takahashi as Grace and a couple other small parts. We did most of the auditions

out of Los Angeles with Montgomery Parada Casting. I was in the room for almost all of the auditions along with [casting director] Dan Parada. I think it's important to work with the actors a little bit during the audition to be sure they can make adjustments.

I wanted Dean Erickson from the very beginning, I thought he was perfect for the part of Gabriel but Jane wasn't totally on board. Dean finally sealed the deal while he was up in Oakhurst and met with Jane. She asked him to do a particularly menacing scene for her and he scared her pretty good. Needless to say, he got the role.

Craddock:	Where was GK2 filmed?
Will Binder:	Most of GK2 was filmed on a stage in Oakhurst California, close to where Sierra On-line was located. It's a beautiful area just outside the gates of Yosemite. Some of the scenes were filmed around the area and on Bass Lake and another lake; I can't remember the name. And the opera scene was filmed in Seattle.
Craddock:	What was the process of scouting locations? What did you look for in a location that made you say, "This place is perfect for such-and-such a setting?"
Will Binder:	Yeah, something like that. Randy, Dave, Gil, and myself scouted the local areas and found what we needed. We didn't have a lot of time to decide on locations, luckily there were lots of great places close by.
Craddock:	Speaking of locations, what was the approximate real-to-movie-magic ratio for settings and scenes?
Will Binder:	The vast majority of the game was photographed on blue-screen sets, more than 90 percent. Location shooting was used for the scene where Huber Sepp's daughter was killed by the werewolf; Grace in the snow for her dream sequence; Bass Lake for the scene of Ludwig drowned in the lake. We filmed in an actual stable for the scene where Gabriel and Von Glower prepare to hunt the werewolf. The scenes where the opera was being performed were filmed at the Moore Theater in Seattle.
Craddock:	Where did you stay while filming on location?
Will Binder:	Most of the project besides the casting was on location for me because I lived in Los Angeles at the time. Pre-production, production, and post-production took place in or around Oakhurst where the stage and Sierra On-lines offices were located. The production rented me a house right by Bass Lake which was great. We did travel to Seattle for the Opera scene and we stayed in a hotel.
Craddock:	I'd like to talk about the process of filming GK2 from both a broad and a close-up perspective. Speaking broadly, could you give us a "day in the life" type overview of a typical day of filming? (Or was there such a thing as "typical" on the project?)
Will Binder:	Coffee with PM Dave Plaskett at 6 a.m. where we'd go over the shot list and talk about the day. Arrive to the set around 6:30 a.m. and meet with the crew and actors and get started. Lunch for a half hour to an hour. Work until 6–7 p.m. Eat dinner at a local restaurant; they had some real good restaurants in Oakhurst. Then I'd go home and storyboard for the scenes the next day and give what I had done to Dave Plaskett to schedule. Then it would start all over

again. Dave and I joked that if the shoot went on for one more week we would not have been able to make it, physically or mentally—it was that grueling.

Craddock: What was the filming schedule for the duration of the project?

Will Binder: The studio was owned by Sierra On-line, and there was another game that was using the facilities. We did pre-production and then shot in the studio for one month. After one month, another game took over the studio, during which time we did pre-production for the next part of the shoot. We then shot for six weeks in the studio. Then the production split into two units, with the Opera sequences being shot in Seattle with Dean Erickson and the opera performers while the second unit stayed in Oakhurst and shot scenes with Joanne Takahashi as Grace Nakamura.

Craddock: What were the biggest hurdles on the project, and what movie (game) magic did you conjure up to leap them?

Will Binder: The largest hurdle of the project was the sheer size and scope that we were dealing with. An average feature film is 120 pages of script. The script for GK2 was roughly 600 pages long. So, in essence, it was the equivalent of five feature films. So we were effectively attempting to shoot five feature films in the same amount of time it takes to shoot one film. Add into that the fact that a good percentage of the action took place in the past, which added the additional complexity of shooting a period piece.

Plus, there was the fact that we were shooting in Oakhurst, California, which is a small town in the Sierra Nevada Mountains. The nearest airport was in Fresno, which was roughly 50 miles away. The vast majority of actors were SAG (Screen Actors Guild) Actors, and were being flown in from Los Angeles. This greatly complicated logistics and scheduling. Actually, the fact that the actors were from the Screen Actors Guild was a tremendous benefit. Virtually all of our actors, with very few exceptions, showed up to the set prepared and ready to work. This enabled us to shoot scenes at a very fast pace.

The way you measure a shooting schedule is by the number of script pages shot in a day. An average for shooting a feature film is four pages a day; we were shooting much faster than that. Over one two day stretch, we filmed 35 or 36 pages, which breaks down to 17 or 18 pages per day. It was tough for the actors to shoot this much dialogue in a short period of time.

We also shot very efficiently. We would try to get what we needed with the smallest amount of shooting time. There are a number of scenes in the game that were actually shot with one take. If the first take was what we wanted, we would move on. Many times, after shooting for half a day, I would sit down with Dave Plaskett and we would review what we had shot and what additional coverage we had scheduled for those scenes. We would concur if we already had what we needed from one angle, we would eliminate shots from another angle and proceed with shooting. This was another reason we could shoot so much material so quickly, by having very little overlap or waste by shooting very close to the bone.

Craddock: What challenges did you encounter that were unique to shooting a video game?

Will Binder: One key aspect of this was the nature of the production being an interactive movie and that the player had the ability to choose which course the investigation would take. The beginning and ending of scenes would have each actor come back to a neutral pose that matched up across the board to give the illusion that everything was happening in sequence, when in fact there were a number of possible ways the scenes could be experienced.

Another aspect was shooting the technical requirements, which were called robots. Robots are shot with the playable characters so the person playing the game can control the character and have them navigate through the playable rooms. The treadmill shots allow the character to continue over large areas. We also shoot robots of the characters moving in different directions like 12 o'clock, 3 o'clock, 6 o'clock, and 9 o'clock which allows the player to navigate the character in all directions.

We shot the lead actors walking on treadmills and in different directions on the stage. We'd also shoot them doing various movements so that the interactive version of the characters could move naturally between the filmed scenes in the interactive game environment. We also shot fidgets, which were small movements the actors performed that we could essentially loop which kept the continuity and the illusion of reality when the characters were in the interactive environments between FMV scenes.

Craddock: After cameras had stopped rolling for a day, what was involved in preparing for the next day's work?

Will Binder: Dave and I would first talk about the next day's scenes and what actors were coming in. Then we'd look at the backgrounds and be sure we had the necessary props and wardrobe ready. Then I'd go home and draw up the storyboards for the scenes, deciding which angles and backgrounds we would use. Then I'd get the boards to Dave that night and he'd schedule for the next morning. When we had days off on the weekends, Dave, Gil, and I would get together at the laundry mat and try to get ahead for the upcoming week while we washed our clothes. We needed clean clothes after all.

Craddock: What factors are involved in deciding the order in which to film scenes?

Will Binder: Scenes were not shot in order. For the first month of shooting, we concentrated on scenes for the character of Grace. At that time in the production, not all of the backgrounds were completed for the game, so we shot the scenes for which we had completed backgrounds. After the first month of production, we had a one month hiatus in shooting during which time the backgrounds for the remainder of the game were completed and we prepared to shoot the remaining scenes.

When we scheduled the order of scenes, we would shoot in such a way that every scene that takes place in a specific location would be shot at one time. For example, there are many scenes in the scope of the investigation where one of the main characters returns repeatedly to a certain location to seek more information or ask more questions. We would shoot every scene that involved that location, even though hours or days may have passed between these scenes during the course of the investigation. This is the way that films are shot, so that you can move quickly and effectively through scenes and locations and shoot the film as quickly as possible.

Craddock: Could you break down the differences between blue screen and green screen? What advantages and disadvantages does each offer, and when would you use one over the other?

Will Binder: Blue screen and green screen are the same process: the only difference being the color of the backdrop used: a blue screen for blue screen, and a green screen for green screen. On GK2, we used blue screen, because the studio that Sierra Online owned was already painted blue for blue screen. The advantage of green screen over blue screen is that the shade of green used for green screen rarely occurs in nature. When you use blue screen, it restricts you from using the color blue when shooting blue-screen effects. Nowadays, everything is done with green screen.

Craddock: What was the process of blocking blue-screen scenes? How did the actors know what to interact with, where to move, where to look, etc.?

Will Binder: We would use pens to paint marks on the floor where we needed the actors to hit their marks. By the end of a month of shooting, the floor of the studio would look like a road map of Iowa, there were so many marks. We would make marks on the back of the cover, or use a c-stand or other implement to give them an eye line to look at off camera, and explain in detail where they should be looking or what they would be looking at in the context of the scene. We had the capability to do mattes of the actors with the background they were working with and we would show them these primitive mattes to give them an idea of the environment they would be interacting with.

For certain scenes, blue-screen props were built to simulate the environment the actors were interacting with. The best examples of this would be the staircases. Evert staircase was built out of blue painted boxes. The studio crew, Randy, Craig and Bob, had done this before with previous full motion video/s and it was amazing the work they did, quickly building environments out of blue boxes to match the backgrounds that had been photographed. For sequences that required doors to be opened, the crew used a metal armature that the actors could push, and then the animators could blend the background of the door with a photograph that had been taken in Europe, to simulate the door being pushed open.

Craddock: What sorts of props do you remember needing to make? Were many of them made on-the-fly, or did you try to stock up as many as possible to keep shooting moving along smoothly?

Will Binder: Many of the props were rented from prop houses out of Los Angeles, especially for scenes like Gabriel's castle and Neuschwanstein. Other props were obtained locally in Oakhurst, Bass Lake, and Fresno. We did build the furnace door in the basement of the opera house that Grace had to open as well as the bridge railing for the scene at the end with Gabe and Grace.

One of the things the studio crew told us that we took to heart was the fact was that it was better and faster to bring actual props in rather than try to replicate props with blue screen. An example of this is the many scenes that we filmed involving desktops. One way to approach this is to utilize a blue-screen desktop and place the props on top of the blue-screen desktop. What the crew had told us, from their experience, was that it was best to have the actual desktop and interactive props brought to the set.

This would save a tremendous amount of valuable production time in not having to build a blue-screen virtual version of the actual desk. Also, the fact that we had an environment of props built for the actors helped to give them a feeling of being in an actual environment, rather than having to perform on an empty blue-screen stage.

Craddock: GK2 evoked such strong emotions and moods. In any given chapter, we'd go from bright and sunny outdoor scenes, to adrenaline-fueled chase scenes between Gabriel and a werewolf, to Gabriel's dimly lit Schattenjäger library filled with musty old tomes. How did you go about choosing a mood to evoke, and then designing these sets (real or movie-magic) to evoke your chosen mood?

Will Binder: The backgrounds for virtually all of the sets were photographs that were shot in Europe and the US. These were shot mostly by Nathan Gams and a few other crew members. The photographs were then manipulated with Photoshop and Nathan added some visual effects to give the sets a background the look and feel of a graphic novel.

One of the werewolves in *Gabriel Knight 2.*

Craddock:	What was the process of working with live wolves? Did you have trainers on-hand to guide them through scenes?
Will Binder:	Working with the wolves was really interesting. They were brought in by professional animal handlers based out of Los Angeles. The trainers were on set at all times. The actors and crew were able to mingle with most of the female wolves on the set and film them freely interacting with the actors, especially Gil Neuman, the actor who played Zoo Boy. But working with the alpha male was tricky. He was very sensitive to his surroundings, and if I remember right, it took several hours before the male was comfortable enough to come out of his trailer.

The shot that sticks out the most is the snarling shot. We needed a close up shot of the male wolf snarling into the camera. To get the shot we bolted a steel anchor deep into the concrete floor of the sound stage. We then cleared the set of everyone except the trainers, Randy the DP, myself and a handful of crew members. A steel harness was then placed around the wolf's chest and back and a thick steel chain was then attached to the harness and to the bolted anchor. Once the wolf was secure, one of the handlers placed a covered piece of meat in front of the wolf. We used a long lens and when the trainer lifted the cover exposing the meat, the wolf went wild snarling and he tried to get the meat. And that how we got the snarling shot.

Craddock:	I'd like to talk about some of my favorite scenes. The first is the hunt club getaway in Chapter 5. At the end, Gabriel hunts down and kills the von Zell werewolf. How did you construct the woody outdoor scene? For example, we see Dean Erickson brush aside branches. Are those real branches, or props? And was the background on a blue screen?
Will Binder:	Yes, those were real branches and bushes that we brought onto the blue-screen stage. Everything that the actors interacted with was real but the backgrounds were photographs that were composited in later.
Craddock:	How did you and your team create the appropriate sound effects and ambient noises to accompany blue-screen scenes? As an example, we hear Gabriel and von Glower crunching across dirt and stones in the woods.
Will Binder:	Some of the sound effects were captured while filming. Many others were added in post-production.
Craddock:	The build-up to finally seeing a werewolf was spectacular. What went into designing the appearance of the werewolf?
Will Binder:	That CGI wolf was designed by Sierra On-line employed artists and animators. When the shoot began, we had discussed different ways of doing the werewolf. We explored CGI, animatronics, and actual wolves. Animatronics proved to be prohibitively expensive, so that was ruled out. We decided to use actual wolves to portray the real wolves in the story, because the werewolf in the story was larger and stronger than [actual] wolves.

At the beginning of shooting, we were uncertain how we were going to portray the werewolf. Because of this, we emulated the film *Jaws* in how the werewolf was shown. In *Jaws*, they used a mechanical shark, but there were so many technical problems with the shark that you don't actually see the shark until later in the film. So we did the same thing: we delayed showing the wolf until later in the story. This served to heighten the tension of the werewolf scenes. So, the fact that we were not able to show the wolf early was a handicap that we turned to an advantage. You could say it was part accident, part design. It was fortunate that we made this decision because the werewolf CGI was expensive and time consuming to produce.

Craddock: How did you go about reconstructing the particular rooms that Grace and Ludwig got to explore in Neuschwanstein?

Will Binder: Those were all blue-screen effects shots, based on photographs that had been taken at Neuschwanstein castle by Nathan Gams.

Craddock: The opera house scene in the last chapter of the game made for such a gripping climax and finale. What was it like shooting at the opera house? It was located somewhere in California, correct?

Will Binder: The opera with Dean Erickson and the opera performers was filmed on stage at the Moore Theater in Seattle Washington. The scenes with Grace, Von Glower, and the Police Commissioner were filmed on the blue-screen stage in Oakhurst.

Craddock: What was your favorite scene to shoot?

Will Binder: That's hard to say, I liked different scenes for different reasons. Maybe the many hunt club scenes because of the dynamics between all of the characters.

Craddock: What were some of the most challenging scenes to shoot?

Will Binder: The final confrontation with the werewolf in the basement of the opera house was very challenging. We were using actual firearms with blank ammunition. We brought in firearm supervisors to oversee that. Nicholas Worth, the actor who portrayed the German Kriminal Kommisar, Leber, had served as a paratrooper in the armed forces so he was familiar with firearms. Also, the CGI wolf was nowhere near finished at that point, so we were uncertain how it was going to look. So that scene was shot with a very much of a fly-by-the-seat-of-your-pants approach.

Craddock: Do you have any scenes you wish you could go back and do over?

Will Binder: There was one scene with Gabriel buying the cuckoo clock that we would have liked to do over. Dean Erickson had a severe stomach virus and was unable to shoot that day. Because the supporting actor was already there, we used a stand in for Dean, limiting the angles we could shoot. The final result could have been better. But these are things that happen on a film shoot.

Craddock: I know filming was intensive, but did you and/or your cast mates and crew find time to bond much, on or off set? What sorts of things did you all get to do?

Will Binder: During the pre-production times, we had a little more time to hang out outside of work but most of our bonding was done on the set where we spend most of our time. Also, Yosemite was close by, so we were able to drive up there a few times. All of the crew members had houses rented for them by the production around Bass Lake, which is in itself a beautiful mountain town in the Sierras at 4000-foot elevation.

I remember that Dave Plaskett hosted some poker games at his lakefront cabin and many of the crew would show up for those. We had a party when we wrapped our first month of production, and there was a wrap party at a restaurant in Bass Lake when we wrapped up production. There was a constant shuttle of actors coming in and out. We would work with one of the lead actors, and various supporting actors would be brought in to shoot their scenes. Some supporting actors were in for as little as a day, some more than a week, depending on the length of their scenes.

Craddock: Who were some of your favorite cast members to work with? Can you share any memories and anecdotes?

Will Binder: Of course I loved working with both Dean and Joanne. I still keep in contact with Dean and just had lunch with him the other day. This is another hard question to answer because there were so many amazing actors and I enjoyed many of them for various reasons. The Hunt club guys were a colorful bunch. Peter Lucas as Von Glower was amazing. Richard Raynesford as Von Zell gave some great performances.

Clabe Hartley, the actor who played Price, had such an unusual take on the character, much different and better than what I expected. He was great. Judith Drake and Bruce Ed Morrow as Mr. and Mrs. Smith were a lot of fun to work with and their scenes were great. Kay Kuter was a wonderful actor portraying Werner Huber. He told us fascinating stories about working as an actor in the early days of Hollywood.

As for an anecdote, I remember the scene—I think it was [during] Chapter 3—when Gabriel visits Von Glower at his home. We shot Dean's coverage first because we wanted Peter to play up the sexual undertones of the scene without Dean knowing about it. Dean was pretty surprised when we shot Peter's coverage.

It really was a great cast, and I think that is a big part of the reason the game still holds up today all these years later.

Craddock: What was the last scene you remember filming for GK2? What was it like saying, "That's a wrap" (perhaps figuratively speaking) for the last time?

Will Binder: I believe the bridge sequence with Dean and Joanne was the last scene where the principles and the entire crew were together, so we had a little wrap party on that day. Dave and I scheduled it that way and it also was one of the last scenes of the game. I believe we shot some inserts, the exteriors in the snow and the opera scene later but none of those were on the stage with the full crew.

Craddock: What are you up to these days?

Will Binder: I'm close to being finished with a feature script, a comedy, that I've been working on with a writing partner. Hopefully we'll get a deal on it in 2014. Other than that, I'm still drawing and painting and trying to spend as much time as I can with my beautiful wife, Hisana, and our two young boys, Alekos and Leo.

Craddock: What did your time on GK2 mean to you?

Will Binder: The time I spent on GK2 was a special time in my life. It was certainly the most challenging project I have worked on up until now. It was physically, mentally, and emotionally demanding, and after going through the grueling process that was the making of GK2, it was incredibly rewarding to see the success the game had and the response from the gaming community. The game received rave reviews. *Computer Gaming World* gave the game five stars out of five, and listed the game in the top 20 computer games of all time.

Later, the game was inducted into the *Computer Gaming World* Hall of Fame. It won numerous awards including Best Adventure Game, The Golden Triad Award, and Best Game of the Year for 1996. The main stream press covered it as well. There was a *Wall Street Journal* article that referenced the game. There was a glowing review in *Rolling Stone* magazine. *Entertainment Review* gave the GK2 an A–. One publication touted FMV games as the marriage of Hollywood and Silicon Valley. So I think everyone involved in the game looks back upon this and takes great pride in the work we did and the results we achieved.

Craddock: Even though GK2 is coming up on its 20th(!) anniversary, so many people look back fondly on the game. What would you like to say to your and GK's fans?

Will Binder: The response from the fans was tremendous. They have created websites honoring the game. They have posted the entire game, all of the full motion video sequences plus the interactive sequences, on YouTube so that people can experience the game all of these years later. There is a website where fans are asking for *Gabriel Knight 4* to be made. This is rare for a 19-year-old computer game. So I would like to thank them, not only for their initial enthusiasm for the game, but for the continued support that comes from them all these years later.

Part II

Ad Hoc

8

Isla Schanuel
User Experience Researcher

If you enjoyed *Into the Breach*'s minute-to-minute gameplay when Subset Games released their turn-based strategy title in 2018, you owe thanks to more than co-creators Justin Ma and Matt Davis. Isla Schanuel is a user experience (UX) researcher, devoted to digging through layers of gameplay to understand the psychology of how users play, what they like, what they don't, and how to coax feedback out of them.

Schanuel spoke to me about her undergraduate and graduate studies in research, the source of her loyalty to Subset Games, and some of the findings she has collected in her work.

**

Craddock: When I think of talking to users about their experience, I think of a community manager: Someone appointed as a liaison between players and developers. How early in your career did you set your sights on user experience and research?

Isla Schanuel: In undergrad I just went to school for whatever would give me a scholarship. I grew up in a poor part of Colorado, and I wanted to go to college. I got good grades in high school, and I applied for CU. I said, "Okay, CU, what can I go to school for?" They said, "Well, if you do this, this, and this, you can get scholarships for it." All right! I guess I'm studying Spanish now!

I ended up with a degree in Spanish, business, biology, and a certificate in digital media. I wasn't really trying for those degrees. That's just what I studied for four years, and it when it was time to cash in my chips, that's what I got. When I went to grad school, that was more of a focused field of study. I studied web design and accessibility. I was kind of an edge case for the program. Their main focus information and communication was technology for development, so even though the focus was on developing, in terms of how it was applied, it was really cool—I've used this a lot in my work—it was about focusing on the user more than anything else.

More than focusing on something for a venture capitalist, you focus on who is the person who's going to be using this thing. If you're building a website for somebody who's poor in the US, you have to understand their Internet connectivity, what kinds of computers they're going to be using, what do they have access to? Whereas if you're looking at somebody from Africa, are you going to get them a piece of hardware? If not, how are they going to access the software? If you're in South America, you need considerations on the physical hardware versus parts of Europe versus parts of Asia.

This constant, three-year focus on who's the end user, what do they have, what are their limitations, and what do they need? That definitely carried over to my work now.

Craddock: Were you interested in games during that time?

Isla Schanuel: Oh, yeah. In grad school, I got to take this class with Clayton Lewis. He used to work way, way back at the Air Force Academy in the early days of computers. He teaches this class at CU which is basically, "Do whatever the hell you want as long as you can defend it, as long as it has to do with computers, and as long as you can do a report on it at the end."

What I ended up doing for his class both times I took it—you can focus on different subjects—was focus on user testing, play testing, and biometrics one time; and I did a little research on virtual reality and motion sickness as well. That was my grad school experience.

Craddock: What led you to Subset Games?

Into the Breach, Subset's follow-up to 2012's *FTL: Faster Than Light*.

Isla Schanuel: Back when I was in grad school, I met my current partner, Michael. He works for Glass Bottom Games, the CEO of which is Megan Fox. She was the former head of the Colorado branch of the [International Game Developers Association]. While I was working at my previous job, I was doing work for her in the evenings, doing QA and user testing for their game *Hot Tin Roof.*

Thanks to Megan, when I got downsized from the job I was working at, she liked the work I'd done and the notes I'd provided for her, so she started asking around to see if anyone else needed my skill set. That's how she put me into touch with Justin and Matt. I talked to them, did some interviews, figured out what they needed.

I ended up working for them for about a week before my father died. They were incredibly supportive about that. They didn't make a big deal when I said I had a family emergency. They didn't ask any questions. I have the highest respect for my bosses. I'm so lucky. I came back after that, started working on the website. We did the full transfer of the website to a new host, worked on moving over their forum.

While doing that, that's when we started working on *Into the Breach*. I've been doing their website, their emails, and doing some testing stuff for *Into the Breach*, help playtest the game and give some feedback on it.

Craddock: What types of tests and research do you conduct to find out what users are thinking about games?

Isla Schanuel: If I had an infinite lab of whatever the hell I wanted, I would do a lot more biometrics, just because I think they're a lot less intrusive. Since you can't really do that in indie games, observational testing has been my favorite go-to. I'll watch people play, and I'll encourage them to actually speak out loud. The best way to do that is to have [testers] be somewhere where they're comfortable.

At my previous job, where I got downsized from and I'm actually not bitter about it. They're cool people. They moved to a boutique model, so they ended up going to downtown Boulder and having this fancy office. It's pretty cool for them. But while I was there, I was working with this great team of people doing the user testing for websites. I'd learned a lot from my job before that, which was working at the University of Colorado on how to make people comfortable in an environment because that was for a language library.

Craddock: What is your ideal testing environment?

Isla Schanuel: What you want to do if you want to get the best results for testing an indie game, especially in the early stages, is make the environment as natural as possible. When I was at PAX just recently, we actually did user testing at a friend of mine's house. We went to his house, we installed the game on his computer, and we had my friend—whose house it was—and one of his friends come in.

I don't usually do this with my play testers, but because these guys were friends, we got some mead. I'm like, "Okay, have some alcohol, sit down, and play the game." Because they were my friends, they were already comfortable talking out loud and were able to give feedback immediately. As they went on, they got more into it. They developed—and I love it when this happens; it's a thing that happens with a lot of play testers—they find what they like about the game, and then they have an attachment to making [the game] better as well.

This happened when we were playtesting *Hot Tin Roof* for Glass Bottom Games. I brought people over to my house and I gave them cookies, and I had them sit down in front of the TV and had them play. About 15 minutes in, I forget who it was, but one of the people we had test it developed a strong affection for the cat companion character. Everything that they said, I was able to put down in my notes because they started giving their feedback on the game as they were talking to this cat.

If there was a puzzle that was confusing, they would say something like, "Well, cat, what do you think we should do now?" Or if the cat was getting in their way, they'd be like, "Goddammit, cat, get out of my way! I need to X, Y, and Z!"

When we were testing *Into the Breach*, Rick, the friend of my friend, at one point stopped playing the game. He turned around and he said, "I think I have a problem." I said, "What? What's wrong? Is there a glitch or a bug?" He said, "No, this game is like *FTL*. I'm going to lose too much of my time to playing it."

From that point on he got really talkative. That's great, because he would talk about his problem-solving process. But not to give me feedback; he was talking to the game. If you can make people comfortable enough where they can talk to the game, just doing their own, personal version of a *Let's Play* or a *Mystery Science Theater* to the game, I've found that's the best way to get their honest feedback. If they feel comfortable they will let you know when they're frustrated, when they're happy, and when they're having a good time. If they don't feel comfortable and you have them in a sterile room, they can't give as much feedback.

When we were at PAX showing the game on a laptop, with Justin [Ma, co-founder of Subset Games and designer on *FTL* and *Into the Breach*], we went out of our way to find a quiet place where people could sit down and engage with the game itself. We could not only see what they were doing, like actually on the screen and see where they're having problems, because we know the game and know how to solve puzzles when they come up. To see other people actually solving them and watching them that way, you can see their thought processes.

You can see, okay, this part of the UI might be confusing because everybody who's tested goes up to this corner looking for this one thing, but it's not located there. Maybe we should move it so it is located there because that's where everybody assumes it is in the first place.

Craddock: What are some lessons you've learned as a research subject that influence how you perform your own tests?

Isla Schanuel: I did an experiment once, which was kind of just for my own amusement. I'd read about something and I wanted to see if it was true or not. I joined a focus group with the intent of getting data for myself. It was totally unscientific; it was just for my own curiosity.

I sat there as an observer and didn't participate in the feedback, other than for what felt natural for me—how it would feel to be in that person's spot. If you haven't been somebody who's done playtesting or user testing [from the vantage point] of the user, you won't know what makes them uncomfortable, or more likely to open up.

It was just for something stupid: pizza. But it was amazing how much the people in the room who had more of a social presence dominated the conversation. I had gone in there hoping to just observe, but I found myself being quiet when people who were louder and more boisterous would speak up.

Some people there had very strong opinions about things like vegetarian pizza. In my case I noticed that the girl next to me, who was a vegetarian, she stopped talking entirely for the rest of the focus group. She would not say anything. She did the hand-raising thing when the person leading the group would ask questions. Up until that point she had felt comfortable expressing her opinion, but this one guy and his strong opinions on sausage was able to make her silent, and they got nothing out of her for the rest of the session.

Craddock: Along those same lines, how do you go about creating an environment where you can get clear, honest feedback from users?

Isla Schanuel: I prefer not to do focus groups in groups where people can influence one another. It's not a natural environment, for games especially. How are you going to be sitting around playing a game and have two other people looking over your shoulder and criticizing what you do? Unless it's a multiplayer game, in which case that's part of the fun and you do want that. You want to bring in people and put them on a comfy couch and have them play [*Smash Bros.*] or whatever.

When it comes to games, if I want to get honest feedback, I want the environment to be closest to how people are actually feeling when they're going to be playing the game for real. Mike Ambinder over at Valve was talking about this once. I read about it in one of their presentations. They were doing play tests for *Portal 2*. In the play test, the reason they knew they needed biometrics is because they had a person who was a stranger to them. It wasn't somebody close to them or in their home environment. They would come into Valve and they had a room set up where they could play the game on Valve's computers.

This person was playing *Portal 2* completely straight faced. Total poker face. He didn't really seem to respond to anything. They said, "Oh, no, we don't really know how this guy is feeling." So they did an exit interview because they had been doing a form of testing where you only watch the player's actions. I would like to do that as well, but sometimes if people are really comfortable they'll talk to you directly. I like getting that feedback. But if you're going to just put them in a room and just watch them as they play the game, you're not going to get that same feedback, and people aren't going to talk to you out loud.

In this person's case, he wasn't responding to anything. He wasn't talking to the computer; he didn't identify with and talk back to Wheatley [character], for example, so they had no idea what he was thinking until the exit interview, which I also do. They said, "So what did you think of the game?" and he said, "It's hilarious. It's the best game I ever played. I was so engaged and had a great time. It's wonderful." And he hadn't even cracked a smile the whole time.

When they had these same people play *Portal 2*'s co-op mode, this person was extremely animated because he was playing with another player. He was constantly talking to the person, constantly giving feedback on the puzzles and everything else because he had somebody to talk to.

Craddock: What types of tests have you heard or read about, but have not yet had an opportunity to implement?

Isla Schanuel: One test I'd like to do that I haven't been able to do yet, just because we don't have anybody I can do this with, is a test that would give me more quantitative data. Most of what we've had so far has been qualitative. I haven't really been able to get any hard numbers on the average time of a match, for example. Matt and Justin can go through matches pretty quickly, and I'm good at the game now, too, so I'm not an accurate gauge anymore.

Neither is my partner, Michael, nor my little sister. I've let them play the game too, to test out new changes, just so I can get some immediate feedback of, hey, I know what this is because I've seen and played it, so here's a new pair of eyes. But those pairs of eyes are the same eyes I've been going back to.

I would like to get some brand-new players in, and I would like to get some solid number data about what the average user goes through. For example, in *FTL*, you have a subsection of users who have never actually beaten the flagship. How many people are in that category? Where do they choke up? What are the problems there?

I would like to know that same information for *Into the Breach* so we can get things like difficulty levels cleared up. What's hard for Justin and Matt might be mind-meltingly difficult for the average player, but we don't know that yet. Meanwhile we've got these *FTL* fans who are diehards. I don't know if you've seen our forums or the *FTL* subreddit, but they're fantastic; they've all got very good attitudes. I want to know what they think about it because they love *FTL* and the difficulty of *FTL*. We want to provide that same experience for them, but unless I [can work with] more than just a handful of people, then I don't really have solid numbers. Without those solid numbers it's hard to gauge where the balance would be for most people.

Craddock: After a test is finished, how do you go about collating data in a manner you or the guys at Subset Games can use?

Isla Schanuel: What I end up doing since a lot of our data has been qualitative, just because we have a small sample size and I can't do accurate measurements, I give them information like the average length of a match for Nick and Rick. Maybe it's been X minutes long. But we can't tell if that's indicative of the average user because it's a sample size of two.

However, what I can do with those, and what I've done in the past in previous jobs, if you have a lot of data from the users who are paying attention to what they're doing on-screen, I will take notes constantly. My handwriting looks like a drunk doctor's, but at least I can read it. I get hand cramps by the time I'm done with one of the tests.

I take those notes, find out what people said during testing, and organize it based on the type of feedback. So if one person had a lot of trouble with an element of the UI, and this was stretched over the two hours that this person was playing, that will be [mentioned] all throughout my notes. I'll re-organize that and say, "Here are the UI impressions, here's how often they came up, and here's my brief overview of what this person's experience has been." It's an abstract, basically, and we see if it's consistent or not with what other players have experienced.

FTL, Subset's first game and one of the most successful indie games funded through crowdsourcing.

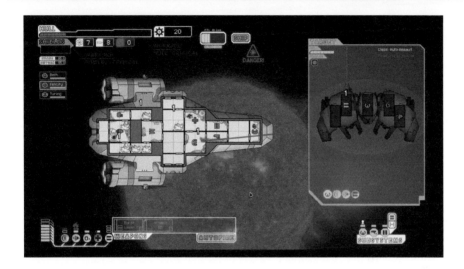

Craddock: As a researcher, you probably gather data you predicted, as well as some that disappoints you. What are some examples of data you found that completely surprised you?

Isla Schanuel: I think the most surprising thing to me, that I noticed immediately, was how excited people get the very first time they figure out how the environment works in this game [*Into the Breach*]. I expect people to be pleasantly surprised by it, like, "Oh, it's part of the charm of the game." But to see multiple people's immediate reaction, to [elicit] some nefarious villain's laugh the first time they push something into the water or against a mountain, that's been a delight and has been consistent with everyone who's played the game.

Even my sweet little sister. At one point, she had a combination where she was able to kill one of the Vek, and push another one into a mountain, and push another one into the water at the same time. She actually pushed back from the keyboard and [burst out laughing]. I expected it from some of the other play testers, but my little sister is pretty cool-headed usually.

Craddock: What tasks do you have on your plate?

Isla Schanuel: Right now I'm fielding stuff like emails, making sure the website is still up to date. I'm doing their web stuff as well, all their web design, and management of the forums as well. I would very much like to do some beta testing as soon as the game gets to that point. I'm super excited about that phase.

I don't know how we're going to do that at this point in time; I don't know how many people will be involved. But to bring in some brand-new eyes to see a version of the game that they haven't seen before, and that we feel comfortable with as a solid, "Here's the game, guys! Let's do it!" To see that reaction from people who have never played it before, I want that so much. I want to do screen sharing with these people, I want to do surveys, I want to roll out all of my tools on this.

Craddock: Since you also oversee Subset Games' website, how does web design feed into user experience?

Isla Schanuel: Mainly when it comes to website stuff, I want to focus on making sure that everybody can read the website. Our website, I will admit, does not look super fancy, scroll-down-and-see-moving-shit-everywhere. But I can guarantee you that if you were to read it with a [mobile phone], you'll be able to read everything.

That just comes from experience. I've had a blind roommate in the past, and I've had friends with disabilities as well. To be honest, as an aside, I think really highly of games. I really love them. I grew up reading books as my form of escapism, but games serve the same purpose. I think that everybody should be able to, within reasonable bounds, be able to enjoy these things. *Into the Breach* already has controller support in addition to keyboard and mouse, and that's wonderful, because even people who have physical handicaps should be able to play the game.

That applies to our website. I want people to go and be able to see what's there without even having to jump through hoops. Things being easy and intuitive. If you have to explain the design of your website to a user, or your game's UI, that's not a problem with the user. That's a problem with your website or your game. The user isn't stupid; they're just expecting something you didn't provide or explain to them.

Craddock: How important has it been to involve the *FTL* community? I imagine they're one of the first groups of users to get excited about *Into the Breach*.

Isla Schanuel: If you haven't yet, please check out the *FTL* subreddit and our forums. I love our community. I was joking about this with Michael, my partner, a while ago: if you meet up with people who play *Dark Souls* and people who play *Nioh*, for example, they're really nice. They're metal heads, and people who like metal [music] tend to be really chill people. It's because they let out all their aggression in these crazy games.

I've noticed the same thing in *FTL*. We have people who have just fantastic attitudes and they're so friendly. Some of the major modders, like Spektor—he did a multiplayer mod for *FTL*. He's very active on our forums. Sleeper Service is also very active. They watch out for everybody. They were the first people who were excited for *Into the Breach*.

The guys on Reddit are another example. As soon as we announced, they immediately snagged the *Into the Breach* subreddit names, so now the *FTL* guys who ran that subreddit are going to be running the *Into the Breach* subreddit as well. I've got to say I have complete trust in them. They have not done anything weird or scary. They have a tight leash on their subreddits, and the forums pretty much self-manage, with the exception of spammers. We get some weird spammers, I will admit.

There's this one existential-crisis robot. I don't know why it was programmed to do this: it just shows up on our forums randomly, with new user names each time. Somebody will be having a normal discussion about mods or a ship, and halfway through I'll see a post like, "How do you know your father exists? You exist, so you must have a father—but how do you know?" I'm like, oh, no! He's back again! What does he want? What is he selling me?

Craddock: What do you have planned for the next stage of testing on *Into the Breach*?

Isla Schanuel: For the beta test I would like to reach out to the existing *FTL* players, especially the ones on our forums. I want to find some of our users, our players, and get their opinions. Not just because they know the game and will love it, but because these are people who I've been watching since I got this job. I've been seeing them around the subreddit, on Twitter, on our forums. It's not like they're friends of mine, but I'm familiar with them. I'm familiar with the way they work and the things they say.

There's a collection of them, especially on our forum, who are very invested in our games and really care about *FTL*. It's not just a game that they like; they care about the game itself, and they care about each other. It's a very nice little community. I would like for that community to be the ones who give us that feedback because I already know that they care.

9

American McGee
Game Designer and Creative Director

Before American McGee became a brand, he was just a normal guy. A normal guy who, at 21 years old, landed his dream job as a level designer for id Software, and got to contribute to *Doom* and *Quake*—games that set the direction of the industry for the next two decades and counting.

As if working for id Software wasn't cool enough, part of his job required him to travel to New Orleans and hang out with rock stars.

McGee is the first to admit that his tenure at id Software was not always pleasant. He'll also readily admit that he has few regrets, if any. If it wasn't for *Doom* and *Quake*, he may never have worked with famed novelist Michael Crichton, bummed cigarettes off David Bowie backstage at a Nine Inch Nails concert, or seen his name turned into a brand with 2000's *American McGee's Alice*.

As part of *Rocket Jump: Quake and the Golden Age of First-Person Shooters*, a book published on Shacknews.com in 2017, American and I talked about those subjects, as well as the kinship he developed with Trent Reznor and Will Wright, how Electronic Arts transformed his name into a global brand, and the fortuitous sequence of events that enabled him to develop his *Grimm* episodic series of fairytale-themed adventures.

**

Craddock: How did you meet Trent Reznor and Nine Inch Nails?

American McGee: When we worked in Mesquite, Texas, we got a fax that said the band was going to be in town, and [an invitation] to come to the show. John Carmack and I were big fans of Nine Inch Nails and we went to the show, but I stuck around for the after-party backstage and met Trent [Reznor]. I think John was backstage that night as well. They also became friends, and I think they're still friends to this day.

Craddock: You mentioned to me that you spent a lot of time with the band. What was that like?

American McGee: It was a little surreal. It was already surreal to be working at id, especially at that time in their history. It was one of the top developers you could be working for. And then the opportunity to hang out, make sound effects, and watch these guys make music for the game was thrown into the mix. I was traveling to New Orleans quite often, which is where they had their studio at the time. It was in an old mortuary, a three-story, very long. It took up half a block in one direction and a full block in another. They had crammed their studio into it, so rooms filled with music equipment, and they'd be having jam sessions, working on either material for a new album, or stuff for the *Quake* game.

I ended up going out on the road with them quite a bit. I [celebrated] at least one New Year with them. I think that was in New York. I also got to know Marilyn Manson and the guys in his band. If you could imagine lots of late nights out, running around the streets of New Orleans and doing all things sex, drugs, and, rock-and-roll. I think there were parts of that that did spill over into normal life, that might have been a bit of a distraction from work from time to time. But I don't regret it now. I can look back and see that if I hadn't had all that fun and taken some of the opportunities I did, I would have regretted that.

I remember moments like being backstage at the concerts, where I was standing just off stage. Stage right, just behind the curtain, and being able to watch Nine Inch Nails on-stage doing their thing, and being so close to the action of it. I remember almost being hit by a flying drum or a flying guitar at one point. I had to duck as Trent threw some musical instrument off-stage and almost hit me with it. Going and exploring the swamps around the outskirts of New Orleans. Talking with Trent about games and life. I got to know him and his story quite well. It felt like he was a pretty inspirational figure. He's a self-made man. He'd gone from being a studio engineer to the lead of his own band.

Craddock: You ran with NIN during the Outside tour in late 1995. I believe that's when they were opening for David Bowie in New England. Did you get to meet him?

American McGee: I remember being backstage once, and asking a guy if I could bum a smoke. I realized I was asking David Bowie if I could bum a smoke. I ended up standing there talking with him for five minutes. I never got close with him, but he was out on tour with the band—either Nine Inch Nails was touring with David Bowie, or David Bowie was touring with Nine Inch Nails—but that was one of those weird little moments. You're a 21-year-old kid who's landed in a job where there's a million other people in the world who might be better at it than you are. And then on top of that, you're thrust into this weird life of rock and roll.

Craddock: What was Trent Reznor like when he wasn't performing? Was it all sex, drugs, and rock and roll?

American McGee: He's a really smart guy, first and foremost. He's a deeply intellectual and emotional person. I think that comes from a past that contained a fair amount of drama and pain. That shows up in his work. When I was spending time with him, I was seeing a side to relationships and adult life that I had never really been exposed to before. I think he was one of the first people to get inside of my head. He was one of the first people to tell me to stop walking around thinking my shit didn't stink.

At that age, I was pretty immature, as I imagine most 21-year-olds are. I got embroiled in a bit of drama when I ended up dating the girlfriend of a photographer. This was his girlfriend, and then she ended up jumping to me. That created a stir among the band members. I just remember him not lecturing me, but trying to talk me through the moral lessons of my behavior. It was interesting because this was coming from a person who, from the outside, you might think was living this rock-star life without morality. Yet there was. There was a lot of depth there. That was one of the things I found quite interesting: He went back and forth between someone who you felt like was potentially off the rails, and somebody who was putting on the act of somebody off the rails.

I got the same impression of [Marilyn] Manson. Manson is another one in that group: incredibly articulate, smart, well-read, and you feel at times, "This [rock-star image] is all just an act." Then at other times you see that the act takes over and isn't an act anymore. Both of them had that going on. It was interesting to be around people who were that complicated.

Craddock: You've talked about dropping out of high school because of trouble at home. Trent had a tumultuous childhood as well. Is it accurate to say you found a kindred spirit in him?

American McGee: I had that relationship with John [Carmack] as well. John is maybe a few years older than me, but if you know John Carmack's story, he also had a troubled childhood. He was reckless, and had some of the same things going on as Trent. I think I drew inspiration from both. I grew up without a father, so I never knew my [birth] father.

I had a series of stepdads, none of whom were all that great as far as male father figures or role models went. It was quite easy for me to latch on to men who projected an aura of having gotten through something and become successful, or at least become whole. That was definitely part of the relationship. I also had the sense, with Trent, that he had taken me under his wing. I felt quite honored to be in that position.

Craddock: After leaving id, you became known for your *Alice* game at EA. Was that your next job?

American McGee: The first job I took after id Software actually wasn't with EA. It was with Michael Crichton, the guy who created *Jurassic Park*. I had finished my time at id and I got a mysterious email that said, "Would you like to come out to North Carolina and come out to see this project we'd like you to work on?" They wouldn't tell me anything about it. A plane ticket was sent. I flew out and ended up sitting in a room with Michael Crichton. Over the course of a year, I worked with him over the course of a year on this project called Timeline, which eventually became a game—that Eidos published—and a movie and a book.

He was another person who was an absolute creative genius and a very attractive individual: super rich, tall, handsome, very intelligent and articulate. That project was what got me into EA because it was Maxis, under EA, that was looking at managing and funding that production. It was a game developer out in North Carolina working on it, and EA was funding them. All of those interactions—spending a year with Crichton, spending my year at Maxis working with Will Wright—set a fire in my mind that here are people who use their minds to tell stories to entertain people, and who made me ask, "How and in what way can the technology we're working with be leveraged to tell stories in ways that rival what Crichton does on the big screen?"

These things were a massive influence, and a massive inspiration as well. At all of these points, I would sometimes pinch myself and think, *Am I really sitting in Michael Crichton's house talking about the next book he's writing and helping him come up with scene scenarios? How the fuck did this happen?* That just seemed to be the path I was on at that point.

Craddock: What was Michael Crichton like?

American McGee: Very, very extroverted. Very self-assured. Very charming. He absolutely knew how to push people's buttons to get what he wanted in terms of asking people nicely to accomplish things he wanted to get done. He had a unique aura about him. At the time I was on the plane flying to go to meet him—I didn't know I would be meeting him—I happened to be reading his book, Travels. It was a midlife autobiography. I was really fascinated with him because I'd read all of his novels, and then my girlfriend at the time finished reading travels and said, "read this." I was halfway through that book when I took the flight to North Carolina. When he walked into the room, I said, "Is this a joke? You're the guy on the back of the book I'm reading."

He was broadly read and experienced. He dabbled in religion, and obviously knew a great deal about science and medicine because he went through medical school. The thing he wasn't good at, though, was computer games. He had a history of being involved with or creating concepts for computer games that failed miserably. In the process of working with him, this was one of the big disconnects and frustrations on both sides of that relationship: The fact that he wanted to do things with games that people in the industry had trouble doing [at that time]. Telltale has done well with their episodic games, especially The Walking Dead. But at that time, the notion of storytelling, especially nonlinear storytelling, weaving that into a 3D environment in a seamless way—the technology wasn't there to make it happen. He was asking for the moon and was getting the parking lot outside of McDonald's.

The Shambler, *Quake's* most fearsome, non-boss monster.

Craddock: You went to Maxis with experience working on *Doom* and *Quake*. How did experience working on some of the most popular games of all time help you at your next job?

American McGee: To be honest, I think I came out of id quite limited in terms of skills that would be applicable in normal game development. We never wrote a design document. By the time I was given the opportunity to build the *Alice* game, that was the first time I'd ever sat down and had to design something. It was the first time I'd sat down and thought about story, level layout, and player progression. We never had done any of that. I was just a really fast and good level designer. I learned how to build maps and make sound effects, and write code, but I had to unlearn a lot. I had to learn a lot of new stuff in order to integrate [at other companies].

Working at id was like working in outer space, and then you have to come back down to earth and relearn how proper earthlings function. I remember on one of my first days at EA, the guy who had helped get me hired—his name is Richard Hilleman—he stood up in front of a board room full of people, 20–30 people who were managers and producers on projects. And he goes, "I want to introduce you all to American McGee. He's come over from id Software, and he's going to show you how it's done!" I was like, "No! Dude!"

But there was this sort of aura, this weirdness of, "Oh, you're one of the guys who was at id." I had to constantly disabuse people of their preconceived notions and tell them, "No, I actually have no fucking clue what I'm doing."

Craddock: The story about your friend introducing you has me wondering about the "American McGee" brand. Did it start there?

American McGee: The name-before-the-title thing was weird, and at the time quite distressing for me as well. We built *Alice*, and because it was based on public-domain property, EA's legal team came back and said, "We're having a really difficult time establishing a strong name for this." Almost every kind of variation you can imagine had been squatted on: Alice in Nightmare Land, Alice in Wonderful Land.

People had done a million variations: as comic books, TV shows, animations, you name it. There was also concern about Disney and the other bigger players out there who operated in the [fairytale] space. The legal department said, "We think it would be safest, from a legal perspective, to have American sign a piece of paper saying we own his name in connection to this [product], and then call it *American McGee's Alice.*" I was resistant, but they said, "Well, we think this is the best idea." I had people telling me, "Don't be stupid; of course you want your name on the box."

I went back and told the team in Texas, *Rogue* Entertainment. And they were pissed. They weren't happy. From their perspective, it was, "We're doing all the work, here. We're building all the levels, we're writing the code. We're operating in the shadows and you're getting all the interviews and all the credit." I said, "Yeah, I understand." I went back to EA and lobbied for that not to be the name of the game. They said, "Okay, if you really don't want to do that."

I thought I had a win. I went back to the team and said, "Hey, guys, I convinced EA to not call it this." They were happy. They rejoiced and said, "Oh, you're a great guy. Thanks so much." Then about a week before the game was finished, I got a call [from EA] and they said, "By the way, we're still going to call it *American McGee's Alice.*"

By that point I had already signed this piece of paper that said they could control my name. I had to go back to the team, and they were pissed. They were like, "This isn't right." But it was too late. I can laugh about it now, but at the time I was distraught. I was very upset. I remember getting on the phone with my creative partner, and him saying, "How should you break this to them?" It made me quite uncomfortable.

But then it became sort of a thing. Fortunately for me, that first game did quite well, and I've got a weird name, so it makes it easy for people to remember its association with products. It's been largely advantageous for me.

Craddock: Since you were at Maxis, did you get many opportunities to talk with Will Wright?

American McGee: When I came out of id, I think I'd been [in a bubble]. There weren't a lot of rules both within the organization and in my own life, I think as a result of hanging out with rock stars. Meeting Will Wright, he was interesting to me because he was like John Carmack in terms of smarts, but with this laidback, California-hippie, pot-smoking, very personable personality. If you can imagine a [precise and detail-oriented] personality combined with somebody who smokes pot, you have Will—quite different, but at the same time quite similar to John Carmack. I would spend time going to lunch with Will, talking about game design and method.

A lot of it his leading by example: seeing how he interacted with his team, seeing how he worked through design. He had an emphasis on design instead of technology. I took inspiration from the idea that a person could have a role within a development organization which was purely focused on storytelling, gameplay mechanics, presentation, and challenge to the player, sort of getting into the player's mind in a more strategic way as opposed to what we [at id] were doing with first-person shooters, which were all about action and adrenaline.

I was only at Maxis there at Redwood Shores for. I don't know if it was even a full year. That was the period when they were working on *The Sims*, so I was going to quite a few meetings for *The Sims*. I don't know if it was only my suggestion, but I know that one of my suggestions was that *the Sims* could pee on themselves. I had some darkness injected into that.

I remember we had a meeting for Sim Mars, which was going to be a Mars-colonization game that I don't think ever went anywhere. I remember being in the room and suggesting that, "Well, if the death of the colonists was going to reduce the efficiency and happiness of the remaining colonists, why can't I have those colonists drive a tractor out for away from the colony, dig a hole for themselves, and get in it?" I was disinvited from design meetings for that project after that.

Craddock: You're still in Shanghai, 12 hours ahead of me, yet all of our interviews have taken place at 6:00 a.m. your time or earlier. Have you always been an early riser?

American McGee: I have been for a long time, especially the last 10 years. The two big projects the studio developed, *Grimm* and *Alice*, in both instances the publisher/funding source was back in the US. With *Grimm*, the publisher was in Atlanta; that was GameTap. I would get up early [because of the time difference] to interface with them.

Another thing is it's just quieter. You can get a lot more work done in the morning. If you go into the office at 7:00 a.m., there's no one on the streets. It's very pleasant to be outside. But if you wait until everyone else is going to work, it can be a madhouse. For me, it's always been nice to get up early and start tackling things.

Craddock: You probably get questions about *Alice* all the time, but I'd like to talk about your *Grimm* series of episodic games. I reviewed those for Joystiq back in 2008, and really enjoyed them. How did that project get started?

American McGee: It was such a weird project. There was a guy at GameTap named Ricardo [Sanchez, vice president of content and creative director for GameTap]. He's a comic-book guy. You'd find him as the executive producer. He called me up out of the blue when I was living in Hong Kong. I was writing a film script, taking a year off and living on this remote island, disconnected from the world and happy about it. I suddenly got this phone call from this guy about a thing called GameTap, which I'd never heard of before. He said, "We want you to make a game. You'll own the rights. We'll pay you based on easy milestones."

I said, "Well, I don't have a studio or a team, but I've been traveling to China a lot. If I was going to do this, I'd want to start a studio there. Would you allow me to take your $3 million and build a studio in China?" And he said, "Yeah, go for it." Which is insane, right? Nobody does that.

I didn't have anyone. A partner, a technical person, a concept artist, no one. He said, "Go for it," so we did. I built the studio and was very fortunate to attract some of the most talented and well-respected animators, programmers, and 3D artists early on. They helped build up the team.

The biggest monster in *Quake*.

Craddock:	I wondered, because the episodes were released in rapid succession.
American McGee:	We could only build small chunks of content. We couldn't build in a lot of interaction for the player because we didn't have the time, so it was going to be mainly set building. That was where the concept of converting the world from light to dark came from. We did a proof of concept of that, and it looked really cool on-screen. So we said, "All right, this is it. We don't know if this is right or not, but we're going to just run with it."
Craddock:	*Grimm's* gameplay was simple, but that's what I liked about it. You just ran around and dirtied this pristine, shiny world, and watched the scenery and characters change as a result. It was very easy to play. I remember just sitting back, holding the mouse buttons to move *Grimm* forward, and steering him occasionally.

American McGee: We were trying to play to strengths. We knew we could tell story, and we knew we had a story. The core concept was the transformation of [classic] stories. And we knew that at any moment, players would potentially start playing in a season that was already up and running. We weren't going to have a lot of time for [developing] episodes, which also meant we wouldn't have a lot of time to teach them stuff. We had to make it as simple as possible, and we were fortunate that GameTap was receptive to that.

What I liked was that from the first episode to the last, the game kept getting better in terms of design, mechanical implementations, what we were able to do in terms of presentation and story. It makes sense, because the last thing you build is the best thing you build. By the time we were getting to the last set of episodes, it was the best stuff the team had built.

As far as the design went, I knew we had a team who had never built something before, working with a technology they were going to have to teach ourselves as we went along—that was the *Unreal* engine—and that we had to start delivering within 12 months of opening our doors.

We had to deliver the first episode, and there had to be episodes coming out after that in quick succession. Twenty-four of them. It was a really insane challenge: Go to China, where you don't speak the language and don't know anyone; build a studio; get your first content out 12 months after you first turn the lights on. But I like a good challenge.

10

Jennell Jaquays
Game Designer and Writer

Right around the time the bottom dropped out from under the North American video game market, Jennell Jaquays was stepping up. Already a veteran designer, Jaquays cut her teeth designing campaigns for Dungeons & Dragons and publishing *The Dungeoneer*, one of the first magazines tailored to gaming hobbyists. Her desire to try her hand at designing and creating art for different types of games—as well as a burning need to earn a living wage—led her to Coleco around the time the leather company released the ColecoVision to go head-to-head with Atari's Video Computer System (2600) and Mattel's Intellivision.

Her mission as one of Coleco's principal designers was to recruit teams of engineers and artists and convert popular arcade games to the 8-bit system. There was just one catch. They were given no code, no art assets, no documentation—no foundation on which to duplicate hits like *Donkey Kong* and *Pac-Man*. To create faithful adaptations on Coleco's notoriously thrifty budgets, Jaquays and her team took the only approach available to them: observe and simulate.

Over our two-and-a-half-hour interview for *Rocket Jump: Quake and the Golden Age of First-Person Shooters*, a book-sized article I published on Shacknews.com in late 2017, Jaquays and I discussed her introduction to tabletop roleplaying, how she became one of the first publishers of a gaming magazine, and what it was like to work before and during the North American video game market crash of the 1980s.

**

Craddock:	You attended college when tabletop RPGs like Dungeons & Dragons were in their infancy. What led to your interest in games?
Jennell Jaquays:	Before college, I played some [wargames]. My friends in high school played Risk, and we did play some of the Avalon Hill wargames. My younger brother was an avid wargamer—still is, actually—so it wasn't until college that I discovered fantasy roleplaying games, or any roleplaying games, because it didn't exist before then. Before then it was just tabletop wargaming. I played stuff like that with my brother; we used to fight miniature battles on our dad's pool table. In

fact, not long after he built it, he never got to play pool on it again. We just co-opted the surface and would set up armies, and have these massive battles.

Craddock: I know some wargamers who enjoy the hobby for the deep tactics and strategy, while others see it as a form of roleplaying. What drew you to it?

Jennell Jaquays: I'd always been kind of a world designer, even as a child. Growing up, my influences were having really cool sets of blocks, and having a lot of small plastic toys. Not as many big toys, but smaller figures. My dad was a model railroader, so he was a world builder in that sense. I got exposed to what he did as a very young person. He was a hobbyist all his life, so just about every single hobby he got involved in, I got involved in, in some way. He read comic books, too, and *Mad* magazine. This was the early '60s. I started reading the comics he collected, finding ones I liked, and I started collecting them. I'd read the ones my friends would read.

I came into roleplaying games with this rich experience of make-believe worlds, and [an interest in] fantasy and science fiction. Later on came *Doctor Doolittle*, a lot of young adult stories about exotic worlds. I used to love that. I used blocks to build those worlds and populate them with small characters. My brother and I each had our personal avatars that we would put into our play. He'd be this figure, and I'd be that figure, and they would be our characters in the world. This was in the mid-'60s and early '70s, before [roleplaying games were prolific].

Craddock: Did you have an avatar that you carried from game to game, or did it change depending on the game?

Jennell Jaquays: A lot of times we played with small plastic animals. I actually had a couple avatars that represented me. I don't have them here at my desk, but I still have them.

Craddock: What led to the founding of the Fantastic Dungeoning Society gaming group at your college?

Jennell Jaquays: My friends Mark [Hendricks] and Merle [Davenport] and I said, "Hey, let's take these skills that I [Jennell] am learning from doing the school newspaper"—I did production on my college newspaper—and [create material for] this game we're interested in. From our perspective, no one seemed to be making material for it. We were all writers and liked sharing our experiences, so we said, "Let's make a magazine and see if anyone's interested in it."

It was originally just the three of us, and then we created an organization that represented [our interest]. There was no organized "Society"; that was just a name we created for publishing. Then we realized after the fact—it's not a thing these days—back in the '70s, there was a thing called FDS: Feminine Deodorant Spray. We didn't make the [connection] between the acronym and ours at the time.

Craddock: What did you learn about campaign creation and storytelling while working on *The Dungeoneer*?

Jennell Jaquays: We only worked on the magazine for around two years. It was less, actually. I'd say it was a year and a half, until the end of 1977, but we learned a lot about creating magazines and even more about how to get a magazine into the hands of people who might be interested in buying it. We learned how to shorthand, how to teach people to fill out a room, drawing maps that you could print. A lot of [what we learned] was production oriented.

We didn't realize at the time that we were making history; for us, it was just a hobby. It was something fun to do, and we found out other people were interested in it and were willing to give us money to do this. [laughs] Not much money, even in 1976 terms, but we were able to do it and make enough money to pay for the printing and distribution.

Craddock: How far removed from publishing *The Dungeoneer* did you learn that yours was one of the first for the hobby?

Jennell Jaquays: Realistically, we knew there wasn't a lot out there at the time. I went to a small Christian college in southern Michigan, and when I lived there, the town I lived in had a big toy store, but it really focused on toys and modeling hobbies; there was no gaming. We used to go up to Michigan State University's campus and check out stores around there. That's when we realized that there wasn't a lot out there for D&D or other roleplaying games. There were some places that stock [material], and we could buy miniature figurines, but that was about it.

So, we decided to make this thing. Later, as I published more and more, there were other magazines out there. And later on, some of them did publish adventure [campaigns]. But—and I didn't learn this until maybe 35 years later—that I was the second. Not the first, but the second to publish a fully-worked-out game adventure in a publication of any kind, and the first to publish a mini-adventure.

Craddock: Is that how you got your foot in the door at TSR?

Jennell Jaquays: Actually, no. TSR at that point was one of my clients. I was throwing sketches at [*Dragon*] magazine to publish. I actually have a drawing in the first issue of *Dragon* magazine. It's not a very big drawing, and it's not a very good drawing, but it's in there. When I left school—I graduated with an art degree in the summer of '78—my first job out of college was doing paste-up [the process of doing page layout prior to desktop publishing] for a local print shop. I'd worked there part-time during the school year, so after graduation I went to work for them full-time.

I was there for a month, maybe two months, and got let go. There was extended sewer construction on the street they were located on. It blocked off walk-in traffic; no walk-in traffic meant they couldn't support the staff, so I got let go. That was around the time I started finding other clients. I worked for Martian Metals [manufacturer of miniature figures with six-sided bases] doing some concept artwork and advertising artwork, and I worked for the guy I'd sold my magazine to about nine or ten months earlier. He was now working for Judges Guild.

At that time, Judges Guild was the only licensed publisher of D&D material. They were starting to publish my magazine. Chuck had taken the magazine with him to the company, and they were gearing up to publish the ninth issue. I had done [issues] one through six; Chuck had done seven and eight; they would publish nine in a new format. I went down to interview with them. They were in another state; that was the longest trip I'd done driving by myself, and I interviewed for a couple of days. They hired me and bought a bunch of artwork I'd brought down. I went back [home] and started working on my first commercial dungeon, one that would be included in the ninth issue of the magazine.

That's how I got my start. It wasn't with TSR; it was with one of their licensees.

Craddock:	How did that work lead you to the video game industry?
Jennell Jaquays:	I worked for Judges Guild as an adventure designer and illustrator for one year. Everything I produced back then—well, nearly everything—is still in print. I was not making as much money as I wanted to. I'll be honest, it was minimum wage plus ten cents an hour. That's all I was making, but I did get health insurance, which wasn't a big deal because it wasn't expensive back then as it was now.

So, I went freelance and started working for other clients. I did that for about a year. I bought my first computer to do word processing; worked with a number of clients both in gaming and outside of the industry. At the end of that year, someone I'd met at a game convention, just weeks before, called me up and said, "I'm working for this toy company in Connecticut. They need one more designer. Would you want to come out and interview with them?" I said, "Sure!" Because I was kind of broke at the time. I'd been working with clients and not making as much money as I needed to.

They flew me out to Connecticut, and I interviewed with Coleco Industries, Inc., and they hired me that day. They expected me to just start working, and I said, "No, I've got to go home and shut down my life back in Michigan." So, I flew back, made some commitments for my life at that point, packed up enough stuff to live out of a suitcase for a few weeks, and moved to Hartford, Connecticut. I found my contract for that job recently. It was for 15 weeks working as a designer, doing electronic toys.

I worked in their advanced research department with [fantasy author and *Wasteland* co-designer] Mike Stackpole. The two of us had come in to design a roleplaying game for a new toy that was using two super-hot new technologies in late 1980: barcode reading, and a speech synthesis chip. We designed the game, and the way it worked is you would create cards and use a plotter to create a barcode that had the faux-names for a word or short phrase on it. So, we could put together a set of roleplaying rules where you used the cards like dice, or to reveal secret information. You fed cards through this reader, and it would say, "Roll 20" or "You hit." We did some other games. We did a detective game where you would try to guess who was the murderer, but with spies, so you could find clues.

We did these things, made prototypes, but when they were done, Coleco said, "Eh, there's not enough interest. Next!" I stayed with them, but Mike ended up deciding that, rather than a career making electronic games, he went back to Arizona and became a famous science fiction and fantasy author. And he did. But I got the same offer [from Coleco], and I stayed. I was with the company from November 1980 through early June of 1985, so I was there when they came up with the idea for the Colecovision.

I was one of the designers of record on their tabletop electronics: *Pac-Man*, *Galaxian, Donkey Kong*—that was the one I had the most input into. The reason I say that is because at that point, I worked with one engineer and was one of the only designers left on staff. We had a cocktail table version of the game, and we sat there and took measurements, analyzed what was happening on the screen. Between the two of us, we turned that into an engineering design that would create a vacuum florescent tube of static images that, when turned on and off, would simulate movement. I drew the production art for that. That's one of my claims to fame in handheld electronics.

But I was there when we started the Colecovision, and by that time the design department had gone through some reductions to the point where I was the only designer left on staff. Because of that, and because I had a good relationship with the department's vice president, I ended up becoming the manager of the group. And then later, the chief designer; and later, the director of design. So, my basic responsibility was to recruit, train, and guide—both creatively and as a personnel manager—all of the art and design teams for all Colecovision and ADAM games that came out of Coleco.

So, a guy whom I'd met at a convention, whom I'd become friends with because he was another RPG designer, called me up two weeks after I'd met him to work with him at a company that, to be honest, I'd never heard of. But they were paying real money, relatively speaking.

A map from *Quake 2.*

Craddock: I'd love to hear some of your anecdotes from that period working on the Colecovision. That was a really interesting time in the industry, especially in North America, when consoles hit their peak and then the market bottomed out. What was it like to work in the industry at that time?

Jennell Jaquays: The interesting thing was we really didn't realize we were coming in at the end. Coleco, as a company, their corporate philosophy was, "See what other people are doing. If it's successful, imitate it for cheaper and make money." That was basically their philosophy. They were a me-too company. They saw Mattel and Atari in the toy market—there was no [console] market at that point—selling these electronic consoles, and they said, "We think we can do that better and cheaper." They were able to create a console that was mostly built from off-the-shelf parts: a Z80 microprocessor, and a TI color chip. That was the core of it: parts that were off-the-shelf and easy to get, and they figured out a way to do it without a lot of video RAM [random access memory]. So, they had a fairly economical console.

They figured they would jump into the market by licensing arcade consoles, because another thing Coleco did was they wanted someone else to presell their work. They liked licensing, and they'd already found out from the tabletop electronics they'd sold that people knew what *Pac-Man* was, people knew what *Donkey Kong* was, people knew what *Galaxian* was. [Consumers] liked the game and wanted to play them at home. That is the experience that, as Colecovision designers and artists, we were expected to reproduce, and to be honest, we did.

Colecovision and Intellivision could do similar types of games. They used tile-based systems, much like the Commodore 64 later on. You made graphics from smaller tiles that you could store in memory. Colecovision had a higher resolution: it was 320×200, which was high resolution in 1982 terms. The Intellivision never got anywhere close to that. It used much coarser graphic tiles. Our graphics system was close to what arcade games were doing. They weren't exactly the same; ours was a lower resolution, and we couldn't use quite as many colors, but we could simulate the arcades. But when Coleco got these licenses, they expected us to simulate the arcade games not only on Colecovision, but on the Atari 2600 and the Intellivision.

Over the course of that period, two of these things are not like the other. We were able to recreate a few games fairly well on the Atari. We hooked up with some super-talented programmers who knew the systems and could make them jump through hoops. For Intellivision, we found people who had reverse engineered it, but it really wasn't designed to [run ports of] arcade games. It worked really well with the types of games Intellivision's designers created for it, but they were creating new, original content that made use of what the console could do. So, in a way, [Colecovision and Intellivision] were apples and oranges.

Craddock: One of the terms I miss from back then is "arcade perfect." I loved comparing and contrasting home ports with arcade games. It seemed like the executive game-design du jour of that era was, "Okay, *Donkey Kong*'s popular. That brings in a lot of quarters, so make that." These mandates often came from people who knew business but didn't follow games. What were some of the tips you gleaned for making a good, faithful console port?

Jennell Jaquays: Most of them were done with the monitor set on end so the scan lines went up and down, so one tip we had to invent for ourselves was, "How do we take these vertically oriented games and put them on a horizontal screen, at a lower resolution?" We would look at [the arcade game] and get best estimates of proportion and scaling, because to be clear, we never got design documents of every kind. We never even got code or [art assets]. Everything we made was created from observation. Observation and documentation.

We had an art team of usually one or two people, and a designer team, usually just one person. They would spend time with a manual stopwatch, wax markers, and measuring tape, and we would figure out what was going on in the game and write up an order that we could give a programmer to replicate that, and to an artist, all to make a game based on what we observed. If there were secrets about a game we never found out in the arcade, they didn't make it into the console port.

Another thing was to figure out what were the most important features. If we had to sacrifice something, what would it be? In *Donkey Kong*, the main map is one ramp lower [than the coin-op original], and the character starts on the opposite side than he does in the arcade. The graphics are simpler. Those were some things: We had to figure out how to overcome technical limitations of the graphics chip, and how much memory we could use.

That was the other limiting factor. When Coleco would figure out a budget for a game, they were looking at Atari cartridges that had 2K or 4K of ROM on them. At that point, manufactured ROM was fairly expensive, so that was one of Coleco's biggest expense points, and they were looking at these Atari cartridges that were really small. What they didn't factor in was that Atari did graphics through timing and calculation. Colecovision primarily did them by using data sets of tiles. We had to store a tile-data set, a color-data set. Each screen had to have an array map [of tile data]. Another map over that remembered the colors for each of those tiles, and there were different modes we could use.

So, we were making a lot of choices about color modes, the amount of detail we could include, the complexity of the graphics. Sometimes, we opted for the most expensive graphic quality we could use; other times we opted for, "Can we do this in half-pixel-block squares?" We did a few cartridges that way. The result was we ended up with larger cartridges, around four times as large, minimum: 16K cartridges.

Craddock: That's incredible. I'm endlessly fascinated by that era of the industry. What are some of your fondest memories from that time?

Jennell Jaquays: Mostly, the people I worked with. Because I was initially the hiring manager for both the art and the game design for projects, every designer and technical writer who came in went through me. I was able to put together a team that really worked well together. A lot of us had come from the roleplaying-game industry, like I had. We brought in people who were writers, and system designers, and storytellers, but we rarely got to make original games. We were mostly doing arcade knock-offs.

The closest we got to original games was making a game connected to a cartoon character license. That was *Tarzan*. There was a *Tarzan* movie that came out in the mid-'80s. I was the designer on *War Games*, based on a movie that came out [in 1983]. We did *Smurfs*. We actually had quite a few [licensed projects]; later on we did a *Cabbage Patch* [*Kids*] games, but most of those were conversions of other people's games.

Craddock: I've talked to a lot of people who got their start in the 1980s and '90s, and one common theme is that teams were small, so everyone wore a lot of hats. Today, you have mega publishers like Ubisoft and team sizes in the hundreds. You're someone who could this, that, and the other. Do you find today that people still need to be able to multifaceted, or have you noticed more specialization?

Jennell Jaquays: Specialization is huge, but it really depends on the size of the team you end up on. A lot of independent developers, if you're on the art side, you pretty much do everything, or at least you need to know how to do everything from 2D graphics through 3D. Programmers need to have more than one specialty: they're not just a gameplay programmer, they're not just a bug fixer. They've got to be able to write engine components, game mechanics, tool construction. The smaller the team, the more general you have to be.

Larger teams become more focused. They're like an animation studio where you have a talent to do a particular thing, but that's all you're going to do at the company: that thing. You never do anything but the thing. If you want to get out of the niche, you have to go somewhere else.

Early on, when I was working at Coleco, we had one animator. He was our go-to guy. He did all the character animation. He'd come from the film animation industry, and he was good at what he did. He was good at getting things to happen with very few frames. But most artists had to do backgrounds, character designer. The same thing for the designers.

The comparable position to a designer [from back then] on my team now would be an associate producer with design responsibilities. Someone who has to get everything done: managing design, communication, all the aspects of working with outside teams. He wouldn't have to be a programmer or an artist, but he would have to be a communicator. That was the key skill. We also had production managers who did bean counting for us and managed contracts.

Observe and simulate—that was our job.

Craddock: Following your tenure at Coleco, what were some of the projects you worked on that kind of paved your path to id Software?

Jennell Jaquays: When I left Coleco, we were all laid off. I was one of the last to be let go from the design side. My wife is over here saying everyone else got turned into *Cabbage Patch Kids*. [laughs] I went to a small, local company that had been started by my first boss at Coleco. The name of the company was International OmniCorp, Inc. Later on, that became Penguin Products. I joined as a design director, and I was there nine months, maybe. It just wasn't working out. It wasn't a creative position, and I needed a creative position.

I ended up being let go. One of the guys who worked there with me had been my second-in-command at Coleco as a designer, and he was just heart-broken to see me leave the company. But I was feeling better that day than I had in months. So, he's crying, he's this wonderful gentleman, 16 years older than me, and was just brokenhearted that day. But I'm feeling like, "I'm free!"

I went freelance at that time, and went back to two industries I knew. One was fantasy roleplaying games. The other was being a design contractor to people who had originally been our contractors at Coleco. I ended up working with a developer who was creating stuff for Epyx. I actually interviewed with Epyx for a design position near the end [of the company] and decided not to take it, even after being offered the job. So, I was working with this developer making stuff for Epyx, and my only design that got produced by them was *4x4 Off-Road Racing*, a truck-racing game. Even though I wrote the design document and a lot of the content of the game, I am credited with "Theme."

Craddock: [laughs] What does that mean?

Jennell Jaquays: Modern historians have interpreted that as, "Jennell wrote the music!" No! That's one of the things I don't know how to do. I had to go into IMDB, where I was credited for that, and change it to. I think it was "miscellaneous" or a "design" credit. But at some places I am still credited with that.

Finding a way around an enemy's shield in *Quake 2*.

Craddock: I didn't realize I was talking to the great composer, Jennell Jaquays.

Jennell Jaquays: [laughs] I know composers, and I'm no composer. But there were other big projects I worked on. I worked on some of my own big book series called *Central Casting*, which were game aids for roleplaying games. I produced a series of books called *City Book* for a publisher, Flying Buffalo, where I did everything for the book except print it. I worked for Interplay as a freelance designer on *Lord of the Rings: Volume I*, which was what they were allowed to call *Fellowship of the Ring*. I was the content designer on that. It ended up coming out on the PC. I worked with EA on the original *Bard's Tale IV* project, which ended up being killed because it was costing too much money, it was not going to make money, and by the time it would have come out, the technology would have been outdated.

Because EA changed their policy for how they worked with outside developers, I couldn't work with them anymore. They needed a full [internal] team. If you weren't a full team, they didn't want to work with you. Raven, up in Madison, they were working with [EA] and got to stay in the family, but I got booted out.

After that, I ended up focusing on art—doing illustrations, primarily, and really focusing on becoming a better painter. I got hired by TSR, the D&D people, as a staff artist. I painted covers and other stuff, including a stint as a director of graphic design. I worked for them for three years right up to the point when it looked like they were starting to tank. I was at a game convention in Chicago during a stormy winter weekend in January, and one of the other guests at the show happened to be Sandy Petersen. He took me out to lunch and proceeded to sell me on coming to interview with id.

Now, the curious thing on that is that 12 years previous, I had brought Sandy out to interview for a position on one of my teams. He wisely refused it, and ended up at MicroProse. Id Software flew me down, and I interviewed with them for a week.

At Coleco, nobody expected me to make a game level. I just went out, showed a lot of the design I'd done. I had a lot of credits already. At id, I would make the jump from being a roleplaying-game designer, to making really interesting maps with a 3D ideology behind them. In fact, that's what I became known for: not necessarily the way I drew them, but the way I could seed them. I was an illustrator at that point, so I knew my way around art, just not around modern art tools and not around 3D [level] editors.

I took a week of vacation I had coming at TSR; that's when id flew me down and I stayed with Sandy Petersen for a week. I went into work with him and edited maps for the week. I learned [the tool] that would eventually become *Quake2* Edit, and made my first *Quake 2* map. At the end of the week they sent me home. That was around Valentine's Day. I think it was Monday before they offered me a job.

11

David Bamberger
Marketing Final Fantasy VII *in the US*

These days, console manufacturers play nice. Xbox chief Phil Spencer, former Nintendo of America head honcho Reggie Fils-Aimé, and Sony Interactive Entertainment's (SIE) Shawn Layden shared the stage at the 2018 Game Awards show, and no one threw a punch! This managed to surprise and delight viewers like me, who grew up engaged in friendly-but-intense playground debates over the superiority of Sega, Nintendo, and Sony.

Things weren't always so hunky-dory between those entities. If you were still a level-1 character in the heyday of Sony's PlayStation, look up the magazine adverts for *Final Fantasy VII* and prepare to be amazed. You'll see bold text calling out Nintendo for using cartridges for Nintendo 64 software, and other in-your-face talk that said, in no uncertain terms, PlayStation was where the cool kids played.

I've spent the past 15 years (and counting) writing stories about how games are developed. I've spoken with countless programmers, designers, artists, musicians, and producers about bytes, pixels, and polygons. In 2017, I pitched a concept to Paste magazine that had intrigued me for years: How did Sony and Square Enix (then SquareSoft) pull off *Final Fantasy VII*'s audacious marketing campaign? How did they land on that tone? And why was it so successful?

Paste accepted my pitch, and I spoke with several marketing executives who worked on *Final Fantasy VII* to get details. My interview with David Bamberger, then head of marketing at Sony Computer Entertainment America (SCEA), follows. You can read the Paste article, "How *Final Fantasy VII* Revolutionized Video game Marketing and Helped Sony Tackle Nintendo," here.

**

Craddock: How did you get started in the games industry, and in advertising specifically?

David Bamberger: I studied marketing and advertising in school. I got my first internship with Goodby Berlin & Silverstein, an ad agency. They were a very small company. It was creative and something I was interested in. When I started doing the internship, I started realizing that in the ad biz, you work on the products that are given to you; you don't get to choose them. If you're not really in love with the product you're [assigned to], it's not as much fun.

I started shopping around with the idea of, what do I want to do? I want to work in a creative industry. In my backyard was Electronic Arts. Electronic Arts had some of their packaging and early advertising created by Goodby Berlin & Silverstein. I don't know if you remember the ad "We See Farther?" That was them. There it was on the wall: the packaging and stuff like that. I said, what am I, an idiot? I should work in video games.

My background is, I love movies. I love Hollywood movies from the silent era, '20s, '30s, '40s, and '50s. I love the marketing of movies. So I felt instead of working for movies, let's work for video games, because at the time I had a Commodore 64; that was my gaming system. I joined Electronic Arts, and I was there for four years. I worked on a number of titles, but I was really interested in role-playing games.

Some of the first games I worked on were *Bard's Tale*, *Star Flight*, a number of ports they had, like a *Might & Magic* game, many 16-bit RPGs. When I left EA, I joined a smaller company called ASCII [Entertainment]. I did that for a while, and then I joined Sony.

Craddock: Take me back to the earliest days of the FF7 project. How did it enter into your purview?

David Bamberger: I'm at Sony and part of the PlayStation 1 launch team. We're working on the branding for the PlayStation and the approach for the brand. In the first year I helped create the brand and launched *Twisted Metal*, *Twisted Metal 2*, *Jet Moto*, and *Jet Moto 2*. Then here comes the second year, and SquareSoft—now Square Enix—shows up. I knew the [RPG] category, and you look at *Final Fantasy VII*, and it was just like, "oh my god."

It took the CG element and wove it into the gameplay. Before then it was used as kind of a thrilling opening, and then you got into the game. Here, their vision was: let's show you the story, and the CG is amazing, and then let's transition to this low-polygonal universe and put you into the game. Even the notion that they had a transition between high-end CG to the more 2D graphics of the game itself was, to me, saying that it was artistic. There was definitely a sense that the people who were designing this game were doing something very smart in terms of interactive entertainment.

That's why a lot of people play RPGs. 16-bit RPGs gave you very little information. They were an advancement from text-based RPGs, but if you go and play them again, most of it's in your head. All that 16-bit RPGs are doing is kind of elevating [your imagination]. I had some of my best gaming moments in 16-bit. Story was key, and I was able to bring that in. So when stuff [from Square] came in, I was the guy who said, "I want to do that. Put me on that project."

Craddock: What's the process of writing marketing materials for a game project? Did you go into the task assuming any understanding of *Final Fantasy* or JRPGs in general?

Final Fantasy VII's critical and commercial success proved to publishers that western audiences could embrace Japanese role-playing games.

David Bamberger: I wrote those documents with the idea that I understood exactly what we had in front of us. The RPG player? We already had them. They would look at this game and of course they'd want to play it. The other idea was saying, "I think we can actually mainstream this. I think we can take this kind of game genre and really get your next door neighbor to play it, and experience what it's like to have interactive storytelling."

That's why you don't see the word "RPG" a lot in the marketing. You don't see mention of the combat system in the marketing. You don't see sarcasm in the marketing. A lot of advertising at that time used sarcasm; they made fun of RPGs and anime to get the mass market to think, "Hey, that's cool, I think I'll check that out," because it was making fun of something else. Our balancing act was, how do you celebrate what this is for the RPG fan, and at the same time attract the mass market to come in and check it out?

Craddock: I remember FF7's box art as being minimal, yet epic: white background, close-up of the back of a character, Cloud, standing in front of a huge, factory-like building. How did you arrive at that minimal-but-epic design?

David Bamberger: That came out of epic-movie marketing, specifically *Lawrence of Arabia.* I'm a big *Lawrence of Arabia* fan, and I got to see the movie premiere booklet. They do a wonderful job of taking shots from the movie and putting them in this high, saturated white placement. They push out all the background stuff for white space, and do a treatment on the people in the movie.

I thought, wow, that's special. It feels prestigious, it feels epic, it's done in the language of movies. I thought that for the mainstream it was important that there was something validating about [the package], something prestigious, and the language you can pull from are things you already know.

Japan had the white box with just the logo. I felt the white box with just the logo wasn't enough information for the western market. The image we chose was for our market. I consciously chose not to show the anime character [Cloud] facing the audience with his spiky hair. That's why you see the back of the character, drawing his big sword, heading into adventure. It gives you kind of a bridge for the mass market to understand it.

The other part of the white box and its look was to create something iconographic that I could use to then create a line look for the other titles in the series that PlayStation had. That was another way to help the mass market find these other titles from this developer. It was something EA did with EA Sports. It made a lot of sense to me, at the store level and within the game. You can see how [*Final Fantasy*] games were cross marketed.

That's the packaging. A lot of it was just creating bridges for the mass market while at the same time elevating and celebrating what the game is for the gaming press.

Craddock: How did your approach to informing games press about FF7 differ from how you informed internal team members about the game?

David Bamberger: That's the other thing. The game had already been released in Japan, so the gaming press was completely aware of what this was. To know that going in was great. The mass media will look to the gaming press to look for titles they feel will make for good stories. The last thing we wanted to do was mistreat or mishandle what we had, which was *Final Fantasy VII*.

That's where the idea of "don't drop the baby" came from. It's about making sure the gaming press understood that Sony understood what they had, and what it meant in the long view. Our PR team did a really good job. The hard part of working with the gaming press was that they had already played the game, so how do they tell a new story? Our PR team did a lot of work, knowing the mass market looked for this stuff, creating unique assets for different magazines. You had an early *Game Informer* cover story; *Game Pro* did a cover story; EGM. That was the media. There wasn't really Internet covering gaming.

Craddock: I have to admit, besides being a fan of JRPGs from the 16- and 32-bit eras of hardware, my primary reason for writing about FF7's marketing was the magazine adverts. They were… bold, in a word. Nearly all of them had an adversarial tone, like Sony, or Square, or both were calling Nintendo to face them on a *battlefield*.

David Bamberger: That's directly related to how we decided what the brand voice was, how we would engage with this audience, and then separate ourselves and reposition the competition. By the time we got to *Final Fantasy*, we understood our voice. We were comfortable when we saw headlines like that to say "yes" to headlines like that.

I think we had to clear it with the ESRB. That was the one thing. They were fine with it. We had "tobacco use" because of one character who smokes. That kept us within a T [for Teen] rating.

There's a great story about the agency. We were seeing early print concepts that made their humor part of the story instead of the game. I sensed that they didn't really understand what FF7 meant in terms of the history of RPGs and interactive storytelling, so I recorded *Final Fantasy IV* and *V*, and also recorded the death scene in *Final Fantasy VII*, where you see the character with the sword flying down and killing the girl.

I said, "Okay, this is what RPGs look like. This is what they looked like just recently. Now, this is Final Fantasy [VII]." You can imagine: it's basically what mobile RPGs kind of looked like: characters facing left, characters facing right, lots of words, and interaction was limited. But people loved them because they were story driven. Then I showed them the death scene, and it's really powerful. She gets stabbed, we go to the transitional scene with the polygonal scene, the crystal ball that represents her soul and her life; it bounces down the stairs and then she dies.

It was like, okay, that's never happened before with a game, where you really feel a character's death. And it's done in a way that doesn't really take over the game from you. It elevates the experience. I sensed that they felt the emotion of the scene, and I said, "Look, this is important to players who love these games. When we show these games in magazines, we want to treat them like [the game] is artwork. We don't want anything on the art itself." We had logos below [artwork]. I think the only other thing we had was the ESRB rating. That's exactly the feeling I wanted you to have: we respect the art, and you can see that.

Craddock: How much of the final result of those advertisements was your choice, and how much was the ad agency's?

David Bamberger: The fun part for me was I was able to pick out the artwork that I wanted. Because it was storytelling, I picked out the hero. It's Cloud moving through the tunnel; it shows a close-up of his face. Then I had the villain with his long hair, and he's holding on to this statue. It's a robot statue, but what I liked about it was it had my villain holding on to something that felt classical. It had kind of a classic sculpture feel to it.

Then you had the shot of the big cannon, and I think we had the establishing shot of the city. Those were the four ads. If you saw all four ads, it visually gave you the hero, the villain, and the place. The one with the big cannons was more a way to talk about CD-ROM technology and PlayStation technology versus cartridges. If you saw that ad, it tells you how many cartridges it would take for this game to work [on a competing console]. That was more of a power-of-PlayStation kind of thing. I wanted you to be able to think you could put [the print advertisements] on your wall.

That's directly related to how we decided what the brand voice was, how we would engage with this audience, and then separate ourselves and reposition the competition. By the time we got to *Final Fantasy*, we understood our voice. We were comfortable when we saw headlines like that to say "yes" to headlines like that.

I think we had to clear it with the ESRB. That was the one thing. They were fine with it. We had "tobacco use" because of one character who smokes. That kept us within a T [for Teen] rating.

Craddock: I wasn't as familiar with TV advertisements for FF7 as I was those magazine ads, because YouTube wasn't a thing and I could pore over the magazine ads again and again. What was your approach to marketing on television?

David Bamberger: For the TV ad, it was very much the same thing. We saw early concepts that focused on the graphics, but the ads we were seeing were… There was an ad that had butterflies landing on the TV screen because [the scene] was so pretty, but it was so pretty that the butterflies burned and fell to the ground. That's memorable and interesting, but it didn't emanate from the game itself. It's not celebrating what the game is; it's not allowing you to see the game.

So they went back and started thinking about that, and that's where they came up with doing parodies of epic movies. We did, I think, three of them. The copywriter is a great writer. He said that when he wrote the copy, he was projecting as loudly as he could to get that epic sound. When they did the scratch track, they hired Don LaFontaine, the voiceover guy for Hollywood movies at that time: "In a world…" You know, that deep voice. He was really friendly with the agency, TBWA\CHIAT\DAY.

We had done an internal launch trailer for the train [commercial]. It had the music that was used in the ad, and was pushing graphics from the game and quotes from magazines. That trailer was something that the Square dev team loved because it treated the game like an epic movie.

I thought the ads were just great. It allowed the mass market to kind of make fun of these epic movies, but at the same time it made its point. They said it couldn't be done in a major motion picture. They were right. And something about, 'You can always hit the Reset button.' The biggest challenge any ad agency has when they're doing television, especially with video games, is the ad needs to stand out on national television against all these other ads and programming. I think we've all seen video game ads that don't seem to live up to the type of storytelling you're getting on television. I think they were able to pull that off pretty well. Credit to TBWA\CHIAT\DAY: they were able to dialogue with us a lot to find a voice and angle.

They made a campaign out of it, which is very difficult to do. You can make an ad that's very interesting, but how do you make the second one? Do you know what you're saying in the first ad that you can make a second one and a third one that are just as entertaining?

Craddock: How much can marketing firms assume a consumer knows about a product? Or to phrase the question another way, how do you walk the line between catering to savvy consumers who have been playing RPGs since 8- and 16-bit hardware, and mainstream who might be buying PlayStation as their first platform and FF7 as their first RPG?

David Bamberger: It was really fun working on that project. You had alignment with all the teams working on it. Everyone was all focused on the same thing; everyone had so much to do to pull it off. By the time we got to E3, it was positioned as a big title, and we were able to do special [promotions] with Toys R Us, with Wal-Mart, with Best Buy. Everyone wanted to have their own way to do pre-orders, so they were willing to experiment with different things.

From the gamer's point of view and from the mass market's point of view, you're going into September, and of course for the holiday season [FF7] was everywhere. You walk into Best Buy and you see FF7. You walk into Toys R Us and see a massive poster in the window. That's what you see from these large campaigns.

You're always working with both audiences. You're working with the easy target and the conversion target. Sometimes you work with the easy target first. You whisper to them. Most people are convinced by word of mouth. You have heavy users, moderate users, and light users. The easy target is typically your heaviest user, the RPG player who's played a lot of these things. You can talk about combat systems and he'll be interested in knowing what makes yours better.

Your job with marketing is to give that person phrases to help explain it to his friends. That's why we started saying, "It's an epic adventure across three CD-ROMs." That's what we would say a lot. That's the plot. If you were to tell a friend, "Hey, you should try to play this game," and they say, "Well, what is it?" You'll response with [the marketing description]. Nintendo will do that, Sony will do that, all the major players. They'll speak in heavy-user talk, but with enough language to help them tell a word-of-mouth story when all the marketing shows up, because a lot of people won't decide what to get until they see it on TV.

The mass market didn't see the print ad. Some of them did because we had them in mass-market magazines like *Rolling Stone*. But most people saw the TV ads. That was the thing that compelled them to get it. Or, a lot of people walked into a store and got a recommendation from the store clerk.

That's another reason the packaging was as clean as it was. If you flip the box over, there's a lot of white space. Not much copy, mostly visuals. That was done as a graphic design. I felt that the prestige feel of [the packaging] would help show people that it was high quality. I wanted it to look like a specialized design that had a sense of quality to it. The company that did that, they're now called Origin Studios, and they had a wonderful graphic designer who took our original art and just really worked it. If you look at that piece, they took a lot of time on it.

That was the idea: have a jewel so after all the marketing is gone and the parade has passed, the packaging is left, and can help people understand the value of the game.

Final Fantasy VII running on Sony's first PlayStation.

Craddock: How did the tone you and your partners chose for the US marketing materials differ from that of other regions? Did you have any input in that?

David Bamberger: I don't know what they did in Europe. That's the thing. I don't know what they did. Sony was kind of easy because you didn't have to do a lot of alignment work with [SCE] Europe, the US, and Japan. There was also this idea that Japan was its own distinct market. Very distinct. So, really, it was hard to divine what these different audiences would want.

I think Sony never really had it in their mind that they would [replicate tone]. At Ubisoft we did a lot of research to understand the gamer mindset between the US, France, Germany, and the UK. For console gaming, we found that they were all pretty much the same. Now, because everything is online, we really do want to have a one-size-fits-all approach, except in special cases like children's marketing.

The most extreme case was _Crash Bandicoot_. They wanted Crash as a mascot, so they redesigned the character for the in-game version in Japan. Crash looks different in Japan than he does in the west. Naughty Dog said, "Sure, let's do this." The game character on the box in Japan is different. That's just what you're dealing with, such as what children's cartoons in Japan look like. You want to align with that because you're dealing with people trying to understand what you're promising. If they reject it because it's too far from their norm, there's an argument to be made there.

I think a lot of it is just picking and choosing what comes across. That's a different east-west thing. I think the US and Europe are pretty much in alignment, other than with sports, in terms of genres.

Craddock: My impression so far is that FF7's advertising placed as much importance on pushing Sony's PlayStation hardware as it did the game. Like they were a package deal: You can't have one without the other.

David Bamberger: This was the one that we felt would help define what our hardware is. This content clearly represented that. The risk was the genre. No one had a crystal ball as to whether or not people wanted to ride around on chocobos, or get into a really intense combat system. Would we generate word-of-mouth among the mainstream in order to get where we wanted to go?

I would say that what *Final Fantasy VII* did for the genre was establish a market for JRPGs. In sports, if you go with football in America, you're going to do very well. Your first market is to convince retailer to carry all these titles. *Final Fantasy VII* created this hockey game for the retailers to understand. It's like Dr. Pepper. It's not Coca-Cola, and you're not going to sell as much, but you're going to sell a guaranteed amount because there's an installed base of users that you know will come in and buy this product.

I think *Final Fantasy VII* created this install base of RPG players. [Other RPGs] weren't going to sell a million units; it wasn't going to be a *Final Fantasy*. But the B-player with an A-game could do big numbers, and it could be a number that Wal-Mart will be comfortable with. The buyers at Wal-Mart don't have to understand the intricacies of the JRPG and why it was different; they just had to say, "That's going to be a good game."

Saga Frontier has so many characters and so many storylines. It's definitely not *Final Fantasy VII* in the sense that you really do have to be a gamer to get it and like it, but it had a very comfortable sell-in for [retailers] because they trusted the brand and the install base. These other companies started coming in and doing very well. I worked on *Wild Arms* and *Legend of Legaia*. I think FF7 really helped cement that idea.

It's not the same market that it was. I got to work on *Grandia II* when I was at Ubisoft. That was a fun project because I was at Ubisoft and this game comes in, and I said, "Oh, I know how to make this work." If you look at *Grandia II*'s marketing, it's an echo of FF7's marketing. Very similar to what we did [at Sony].

Craddock: It seems like the tone and stance you chose for FF7 helped position PlayStation in a field where Nintendo and Sega already had a lot of space and goodwill from consumers.

David Bamberger: If you go back and look at video game hardware branding, Nintendo was speaking to a target [demographic], probably 12- or 13-year-olds. In marketing there are often voices that you can own. You can think about Disney: they own the family, inclusive voice. That's all part of their logic and messaging. Then you have Nickelodeon. Knowing their position against Disney, they'll take the more the-parents-are-outside-the-circle stance, and children are all-knowing and all-seeing. Both brands know that and actively make sure that separation is there. Cartoon Network comes in and has to find a different angle.

Nintendo is the inclusive, family-friendly, multi-generational brand. Sega comes in and says, "There's no way we can be that because the world already has that, so let's create our brand to be this challenger, this more rebellious brand." When you look at marketing from the 16-bit period, it has a certain silliness to it. "SEGA!" Or you have pictures of people looking very close at the camera, their eyes are big and really silly.

That's the way that Sega Genesis branded itself, and continued to brand itself even though the market was getting older. At EA, they had so many games. They had a big deal with Sega allowing them to publish as many games as they could, and this amazing sports franchise [*Madden NFL*] that allowed them to attract this broader market.

When we started branding PlayStation, we were going, "Well, I think the goal should be to replace Sega Genesis in the market." Their market share was getting older; the median age was getting older. Then we could expand to [focus on] Nintendo. The overall strategy was to go out and replace Sega so that the people left standing would be Nintendo and Sony.

Now, how to speak to the older audience in a way that's different and just as compelling and relevant? To reposition Sega as younger than Sony? CHIAT\DAY and really smart people at Sony, the VP of marketing, worked really hard at understanding the audience, understanding attitudes about Sony, attitudes about Sega, and came up with a brand platform that made the median age of whoever's playing this game 18. If you're 25, you play 18 again; if you're 13, it's an aspirational brand.

We argued that the Genesis brand was probably 13. The way they spoke to you, they told you how to feel. They gave you the punchline. They were silly, and it was self-evident that they were silly. Their sense of danger wasn't adult dangerous; it was more adolescent danger. We actively went after this tonality of interactive communication. We would put challenging things out there to let you think about what we just said, and we tried to find what we called "adult dangerous" topics.

That was at launch. You probably remember, "You are not ready." That was an interesting slogan because that basically denied you the technology. It told you, "Whatever you're playing, you're not ready for this." We knew people really respected Sony's technology, so we used that as a way to say, "Hey, you're not ready for this. This is a little too advanced." A lot of the ads we did really early on dealt with how this game [console] was going to own you. Unprecedented challenge was what this system would deliver you because it had 3D, and it had all this tech.

That's your first year. I think the team—TBWA\CHIAT\DAY, the marketing team at Sony doing all these campaigns—we did *Twisted Metal, Crash*

Bandicoot. We had *Crash Bandicoot* with a bullhorn yelling at Nintendo [of America] in their parking lot. It was like, I can't believe they're doing that! A man on the street, yelling at Nintendo with a bullhorn!

That was all part of the idea that we would do things that were dangerous that adults could do. We learned what that meant. We learned what was the difference between crude humor and dangerous humor, and we started building this tonality. Then these games showed up, like *Final Fantasy,* that were going for an epic tone and a serious tone. *Bushido Blade,* same type of thing. And we were primed for it because we trusted [our brand]. By that time we had really good synergy, conversation, and energy with the creative teams at TBWA\CHIAT\DAY. That takes time.

This was still year two. Nintendo had habit, loyalty, and awareness. A lot of that came down to, what is the market size? What can we do with this? Anytime you [prepare to market a product] you do an analysis. It's called a slot analysis. You do a slot, and you look for things. You play devil's advocate. I think the thing that stood out for us was we really didn't have an RPG in what we had available. I can't remember what we had for the first year for PlayStation.

Sega Genesis had a number of RPGs, but you always knew how many you could sell. Nintendo was the king because they had Square, they had *Dragon Quest* [from Enix]. But my god: Nintendo, right? *Secret of Mana? Great game.*

I don't know if [FF7's campaign] was a culmination. It was just perfect timing. We were really taking off, and starting to get headwind. The Sega products were distancing themselves [from older consumers], so we definitely hit our stride, and it was to the benefit of [*Final Fantasy VII*] that it came around when it did. We'd already done a number of large, complex launches, especially launches that had ship dates tied to them. Event launches.

Craddock: When does marketing for a game end? Is all of your effort concentrated on launch day?

David Bamberger: We also got really good at building the kind of campaigns that you need in order to generate that level of demand. Part of what you saw in my marketing campaign was a 12-month campaign to generate the level of interest, demand, et cetera to deal with the logistics problems of plastic goods. How do you get a game to sell through a million units at the time we were trying to do it? A lot of that is, you build your case slowly over time, like a drumbeat.

One of your biggest challenges of getting an RPG to that target was convincing Wal-Mart, Target, Best Buy... Not so much GameStop because they knew about RPGs. It was more the mass market retailers, to get them to understand. Their sense of what RPGs were was a much smaller volume. Once they heard "RPG," they could go, "Okay, this is the volume that, historically, that we can get out of this type of product, so we'll pick up this many for our first order."

Your first order goes in, it sells through, and everybody's really happy. But if you do the math, your starting number will then dictate what your life time number is going to be. You have to build a case to get that starting number to a point where when you do your real order, you can get to that bigger number. This is why you saw Activision, Ubisoft, EA, [bigger publishers] talking to retail a year and a half before big releases. They have to build their case.

For *Final Fantasy VII*, we started a year before release. We then sent a lot of internal documents saying, "This is our tent pole." Triple-A. That's what we called it. In the movie industry, you have tent pole films, those that will make or break a studio for a given year. This was our tent pole, and we started treating it that way.

Craddock: So, we've covered magazines, ads, the press, and consumer messaging. What part do retailers play? For example, when I walk into GameStop or Target, sometimes I'll see huge cardboard standees in the shape of a game character or setting.

David Bamberger: We would do a press event, and we'd gather a lot of the things you want to hear that make these things a slam dunk to retailers, and make sure it was always in that prestige, triple-A bucket for the retailer. That way they know, "Okay, that's the big one." Over the course of the year they show up to E3, and they can see that we dedicated an area for it, and we're showing off a big, beautiful area of [the game]. That reinforces what the title is doing. Then you take them through the marketing campaign, and it's very creative and epic. It's not one print ad, it's four. It's not one TV ad, it's three. It's a promotion with Pepsi.

We did a massive promotion with Pepsi where there was a 15-second ad that was at the end of football games that talked about the special packaging that featured game characters that were big hits for the holiday season. One of them was *Final Fantasy*.

You also had a lot of in-store merchandise to make available to [retailers]. That's another indicator to them that this [game] is a big deal. One thing that's interesting packages to marketing is that I can tell you that it exists. There are two kinds of targets. There's an easy target in the sense that it's easy to convince an individual that [a product] is something they want. Then there's the conversion target, where you need to make a very good argument and back it up so that you're not only aware of it and interested in it, you actually do something about it. You go to the store and buy it. That's a big step.

Part of the reason you have in-store merchandising is that it helps validate to that conversion target that, okay, this is the one they've got to get. That was part of our mass-market [appeal], too. We had a beautiful standee of Cloud holding his sword that was pretty tall. I want to say it was four feet tall. That was more of an enthusiast piece we did for GameStop stores. It was a [display] that had Cloud, and four other games coming out, all in one stand. I think it was *Final Fantasy [VII], Bushido Blade, Saga Frontier, Final Fantasy Tactics.*

FF7 was another example of how the line created coattails for these other titles for Square, and helped *Final Fantasy Tactics* attract more people. It didn't post *Final Fantasy VII* numbers, but it sold well above what other strategy games had performed at prior. It was front loaded: you were aware of it when you got FF7.

Craddock: So much of marketing involves preparation. What happens when plans go awry?

David Bamberger: That's an interesting story. We almost missed that launch because the game stopped working. We were basically done, through QA, all done. They had the final discs, the gold masters. And they wouldn't load. There was silence at first; like, "Huh. Why is that? I don't know." Everyone just took a collective breath and let the tech guys go off into the wilderness and think about what would stop this thing from loading.

It was somebody not working on the project [who solved the problem]. It was one of our tech guys who reasoned that it might have been because of the way the videos were loading in. Something about the tech in the videos. Over the next couple of days—it was the weekend—he had the idea and sent it to the dev team. The dev team made the change, and lo and behold, we were back on schedule. It was one of those moments where you go, we're wound up, teed up; everything is ready to go. [Materials were] printed with the ship date.

What I loved about that is that no one panicked. Everyone just let it ride because we had a little bit of a window. It was one of those things where if they couldn't figure it out, we were that close to having to [reconfigure] the ship date schedule.

You have to do manufacturing, so you had to gold-master the code and give it to production so they can create all the game [discs]. You have to then ship them to all the different stores to make the ship date. So you have a D-Day, and you work backwards from that. It was close enough to, we have to start making these games now, to where it was urgent.

Craddock: Every piece of advertising makes a promise, right? Even if it's not implicit, marketing materials are saying, "You need this product, and you'll love it." How do you help make sure your materials align with the product to deliver on that promise?

David Bamberger: In this industry, because you have such a passionate base, if you make a promise that you can't back up, or if you overpromise, you hurt people's feelings. It's a very serious business to the people who really care about these games. We've all seen marketing campaigns that have overpromised. In marketing we talk about consumer promises: "I promise you this." The way you talk about it is, "I understand something about what you're missing or what problem you have, and I can fix that. I promise you that I can do X-Y-Z. You can believe this promise because…"

The marketing task is to figure out what they want and need. Then it becomes a development challenge, because you want your promise and what your game is delivering to basically be the same thing. Ubisoft has done a wonderful job of getting ahead of that if you look at *Prince of Persia* and *Splinter Cell*. For the longest time they did *Rayman*, then a whole series of games that weren't very good. I was at Ubisoft for six years where we were doing *Rayman* games and not-very-good games.

Then there was a revolution led by the head of that company, Yves Guillemot, in how to better engage with the needs of the players. That put Ubisoft in a position to meet that need. It was done very consciously, in a way that integrated how marketing talked about things, how production talked about things, and how executives green-lit ideas, and how they then created franchises.

I love stories like that because it shows you the genius of the system. To do something and rise up as kind of a backwater publisher to a top-three publisher—that was one of their big goals: "We want to be top five by 2005." That was the rally cry.

It gets to this idea of consumer promises and simplifying the message in a way that you can cut through the clutter. That's the other part. How do you create difference in your game? How do you stand out? *Twisted Metal*, in terms of marketing, was interesting. How do you position a game within a corporation to where it's seen as a hardware driver? At the time of *Twisted Metal*, they didn't have this rebellious product. To actively position the title that way allowed the company to say, "Maybe this title could be a pillar." That invited more interest, more marketing, more ability to be a part of commercials and television.

How do games rise up in these big organizations? That's another story.

12

Chris Ansell
Marketing Final Fantasy VII *in Europe*

If you read the earlier chapters of this book before arriving here, you know I set out to learn how Sony and SquareSoft devised a bold and ingenious marketing campaign for *Final Fantasy VII*. (And if you didn't read the chapters in order, you're a monster. Just kidding! You should go back and read David Bamberger's interview, though.)

TV and print advertisements hit all the right notes: playing to the idea of "console wars" between Sony and Nintendo—notice how Sega was an afterthought?—and showing off the then-jaw-dropping technical power of the PlayStation.

The first chapter covered my interview with Sony Computer Entertainment America's (SCEA) David Bamberger. In this chapter, I present my full interview with SCEE's (Europe) Chris Ansell, who speaks to how SCEE's approach differed from SCEA's.

**

Craddock:	How did you get started in the games industry, and in advertising specifically?
Chris Ansell:	I completed my bachelor's degree in economics, focused on marketing in Sydney, Australia. I knew that I wanted to work on something that I truly loved as opposed to falling into any old marketing job. I didn't particularly want to market something I had no passion for because both my parents had followed their passion and did very well. That was the model I was lucky enough to be given.
	I was playing tennis one day and simply had a brainstorm. What do I love? Video games. What's the hottest new thing? PlayStation. From reading *Edge* magazine and knowing all about it, I was very excited about it: CD-ROM, et cetera. I contacted the Australia office for PlayStation, and at the time they had about six employees to handle [the brand] for all of Australia. I knew that was way too small. They were kind of hidden within the Sony Music building in Sydney, and I offered to do a week of free interning for them.

They were looking for people to help, and it turns out they didn't have anyone at the time—this was very early—who knew about the games in detail, the launch titles. I knew everything about them: *Battle Arena Toshinden* and all that. I basically got in there and tried to make myself as indispensable as possible, put my name on every single document and just worked my ring off to show there was a viable need for someone to help with the PR for the actual games.

About a week and a half later they gave me a call and said, 'We need this role. Would you come in?' I was pretty much the happiest guy on the entire planet.

Craddock: Take me back to the earliest days of the FF7 project. How did it enter into your purview?

Chris Ansell: That's a huge story. I wasn't particularly exposed to any of that direct, sort of exec-to-exec discussion. At the time I had just moved from the Sydney office to London, SCEE's headquarters. They asked me to be a product manager, so I moved into marketing from PR. I was lucky enough to work on *Final Fantasy VII*'s launch in Europe. It was very, very exciting.

I learned more of the details on that business deal and how Sony worked some magic to bring Square across from Nintendo to the PlayStation fold. Obviously things like the CD-ROM, its capacity for FMV and its increase in visual fidelity, all of those things played to [Hironobu] Sakaguchi-san's vision for where he wanted to take[*Final Fantasy*] *VII*. There were obviously discussions behind closed that I simply wasn't privy to, but we were happy to have Square's stable of products, starting with FF7, come to PlayStation.

That's really where I also fell in love with turn-based RPGs and JRPGs. It was a big education for me, as it was for most of European mainstream gamers.

Final Fantasy VII.

Craddock: What were some of the unique challenges of marketing an RPG in Europe versus any other audience you'd worked with?

Chris Ansell: I'm just positing, but you had a very strong passion across Europe for established genres like football, or soccer; action games like *Tomb Raider*, arcade shoot-em-ups and fighting games. There hadn't really been any publisher who had luck with or insightful ways to translate and kind of [communicate] JRPG benefits in a way that would make sense to a European audience.

Also, I think maybe they had a niche appeal. A lot of consumers maybe hadn't bought them, so they remained in Japanese, and I'm sure publishers were running the numbers of the cost of localizing JRPGs in five or six languages across Europe, and maybe the numbers didn't make sense at the time. It was a case of the chicken or the egg. I think with *Final Fantasy*, the incredible visuals in the FMV, which we heavily focused on in the marketing, were kind of the tip of the spear, the head of the ram, that kind of showed everyone, "Wow. Okay, this is amazing." It was almost like a sugar coating that people really needed in order to get brave and try it.

Craddock: What was the level of collaboration between Sony Computer Entertainment America (SCEA) and Sony Computer Entertainment Europe (SCEE)?

Chris Ansell: It was very collaborative. My team and I in [SCEE] were working with Square's marketing and publishing division in Tokyo. We were working very closely. A lot of importance was placed on making sure it was a flawless execution for European audiences to catch people up on what *Final Fantasy* meant to so many players in so many parts of the world, and what it could to players who hadn't really experienced it yet.

We worked very closely with Square's Japanese team on the marketing side, and they also worked closely with the US marketing team at SCEA. We'd sometimes collaborate with those guys as well. They might develop a certain look, such as covers or key art, and we might take some of those elements, or vice versa.

You always want to tailor the marketing's messaging, tone, and visuals to your specific audience. That generally lent to different assets being created, different tones and styles being produced for European players versus in North America.

Craddock: I've talked with David Bamberger, who was at SCEA for FF7. We talked extensively about how the marketing tone for FF7 over here was very aggressive. Did you want to take a page out of that playbook for Europe?

Chris Ansell: We weren't quite that aggressive. We worked with the folks at Square to find out what they were looking for because they were so close to the title. We really took a lot of cues from the incredible atmosphere, like the transformative visuals they had. My memory might be fading in some parts, but we absolutely fell in love with the key images around Midgar. There were some beautiful renders of Midgar, with all the incredible exhaust ports and smoke stacks in that circular pattern. That was so epic because the render quality was just a level above.

We gravitated toward the incredible environments, which also spoke to the graphics and what the PS1 could do through FMVs. Also, we really wanted to push the characters. I remember for some poster layouts and in-store retail layouts, we took the [Midgar] city image, and we had a great graphic design team. We took some of those smoke stacks and smoke and kind of extended them upwards vertically, which led into Cloud's face, Aerith's face, and Barrett's face emerging in the clouds. We loved to play with a lot of the beautiful key renders and play them up, just really sell a cinematic experience that you'd never played before. The FMVs really helped us do that.

Craddock: Part of the US campaign's strategy was an "us versus them" mentality between Nintendo, primarily, and Sony. Did you want to buy into the console wars with your marketing?

Chris Ansell: I think as long as there's been consoles, even back in the '70s when I was playing Intellivision, kids have looked for something to argue and fight about. There's always a proxy. I think consoles have been great for that. I did it as a kid, and I think every generation of kids with their console wars has done it.

One of the things that I've done with previous titles, with *Prototype*, is there's so much natural and kinetic energy in the console war. Teens, 20-year-olds, 30-year-olds and above, arguing why their console is better than the competitor's. We've tried in the past to insert our product, and stand it on top of that existing fight. It's fantastic from an awareness point of view if someone can't mention PlayStation or Xbox without also mentioning the title you're promoting as an example.

We were certainly having a lot of fun, and I'm sure the guys at Sucker Punch were, when we did the *Prototype* versus *InFamous* campaign, because it was impossible for any Sony fan to mention *InFamous* without [also] talking about *Prototype* and vice versa. We kind of leaped into that existing, back-and-forth, competitive energy. That's certainly a strategy: inserting your product into an existing conversation.

Craddock: What other challenges did you encounter as marketing development got underway?

Chris Ansell: A big challenge was making sure we had press get their hands on it, and consumers at the events we were attending, so they could see how the FMVs blended into the turn-based, isometric-perspective graphics, because obviously there was a major difference there. But even at the time the isometric graphics were beautiful. It was some real eye candy, just to be moving your characters around those environments.

Craddock: You mentioned RPGs not being as popular in Europe. What steps did you take to reach consumers?

Chris Ansell: The marketing budgets were very healthy for all the different territories across Sony. It was very important that we made a smash hit out of publishing Square's first title [with Sony]. Nothing was held back. We were hitting

TV, double-page printing ads, the front pages of newspapers across France, Germany, Ireland, England. We had giant, outdoor billboards that you see on the sides of freeways. They had consistent key-art messaging.

We used the logo, of course, plus the beautiful environments and characters. We really approached it like we were marketing a film. That was a big thing from the very start: to market the game like Sony Pictures would market a blockbuster, tent pole release. At the time, there wasn't a lot of that kind of thinking. Now you sit in any marketing meeting for any publisher in the AAA space, and you can play buzzword bingo: "We're going to market this like a tent pole film release." You hear that every day, but at the time it was very novel.

I remember in the PowerPoint slides in presenting the strategy to Square, we had a lot of film canisters in the room, we had movie-director chairs, just to make that immediate impression of, this is how we want to approach this because it's just so beautifully cinematic and will sweep players away. It will be a completely different experience than you can find anywhere else. That was a huge part of mass market appeal using those notes, those tones that consumers would see regularly and attaching them to giant films.

Craddock: Since FF7 was already out and popular in Japan, did Square provide any support or direction for marketing in your territory?

Chris Ansell: I remember sitting with the head of marketing of Square Japan. He provided great guidance and assistance as to what he wanted to see in the launch trailer, the announce trailer, the kinds of scenes that would be great to show and that they wanted to keep secrets. We didn't have Reddit, forums, and Twitch back then, but it was still very much a consciousness to hold secrets back and just show enough to get people's appetites whetted.

I certainly remember long hours, Soho AB's studios, working with the editors on trailers, working with design agencies. The artwork was incredible. It's a dream for a marketer to receive organized, well-documented and detailed from all angles, key character art, environment art, CGI renders— which back then were still a luxury. Honestly, Square had such a big team working on those sequences; they were just mind blowing.

We had a wealth of stunning imagery, and that made things a lot easier in terms of putting together a campaign on a month-by-month series of beats that led to our cohesive message of why you needed to buy this game, just by first seeing those incredible assets that were coming across by FTP from Japan.

Craddock: Today, there are all sorts of metrics to measure marketing's impact on sales, namely social media hashtags, likes, shares, that sort of thing. How did you rate the impact of your advertising on sales?

Chris Ansell: All signals were that it was incredibly overwhelming. The game sold so much, way beyond our expectations. We had strong expectations, and even way beyond that—especially in Europe, where we had to gamble on, you know, will a turn-based JRPG take off when they haven't done that well in the past? What would the response be to it being such a giant, long game?

I mean, it was massive. Would people have the patience to sit through it all and enjoy it?

At the time we could track things like TV viewership on the ads. Obviously we had some in-house and external agencies tracking that. All the metrics were incredible for seeing the ads because of the incredible CGI, of course. We made sure to really focus on the logo and the core compositions. It was a grand slam, sort of hat trick for us when it came to reviewing the spend versus the actual result.

A battle in FF7.

Craddock: Of all the materials you worked on, which was your favorite?

Chris Ansell: My immediate thought is, we worked with an incredible design agency called Fluid. Just a fantastic team. One of their designers came up with the concept of taking the Midgar render, the sort of circular design of it, and extending up the smoke effect all the way up so it was a long, vertical poster, and then you had the three protagonists' faces emerging from the smoke. It was just fantastic. It was such a good way of combining the environment, and the story it told by itself, with the characters into something like a film poster.

I remember Square Japan absolutely loved it. That was awesome. We could take that design as our key piece of art, and then we would spin that out into all the different shapes and sizes of assets over the campaign and territories as needed, because every territory across Europe—France, Italy, Germany—everyone's its own separate market in terms of what the retailers need, what the press needs, what the PR and marketing teams require for them to be successful. That was the one piece that when we nailed that, I knew we had the perfect piece of key art.

Craddock: One reason I'm writing this article is because I don't think many people consider the impact marketing can have on a game, and on the industry at large. You really only hear about marketing when a commercial or ad is cheesy or bad. FF7's marketing campaign was so memorable. What impact do you think it had on games marketing? How has it influenced your work on subsequent projects?

Chris Ansell: I do think that made a definite impact. Obviously it was tougher for competitors to fully embrace what we did with the campaign because there weren't many game studios able to commission epic, CGI sequences. It was exorbitantly expensive, and not many people knew how to do it well at that time. I do think it certainly opened publishers' eyes to, wow, we can go that route. Now the games industry is still learning to walk, I think. It's probably a teenager in terms of its relative age to other industries. But at the time it was still in its infancy, and I think it was a big turning point for realizing, wow, we can be more aggressive and confident in what we're producing.

As graphics were [evolving], it did open up the chance to make that connective tissue into messaging like what others were doing in film. We could show off graphical fidelity more and not be so afraid of it. There's always been a tendency, as you could see in the early '80s from Nintendo's ads, you tended to see advertising that was all about kids playing in the living room and throwing their hands up in the air, and the screen would be hard to see because there wasn't anything really sexy about 8-bit graphics.

This was the first time that you had Hollywood-quality visuals that could be used in the messaging for a game. It was certainly ahead of its time, and it showed publishers that it could be done. It certainly paved the way for more of that tent pole marketing in video games.

13

Brian Harvey
Educator

I conducted dozens of interviews to write *Dungeon Hacks*, my 2015 book about the making of formative roguelikes such as *Rogue, Beneath Apple Manor, Angband, NetHack*, and *ADOM*. Of all the conversations I had, my asynchronous chat with Brian Harvey, conducted over email, was one of my favorites.

Brian is an articulate and fun-loving teacher whose student-first philosophies made it possible for a group of kids in his first computer class to learn about programming through experimentation. That environment, in turn, made possible the advent of *Hack*, a *Rogue* clone created by those same students. The domino effect continued when the kids distributed *Hack* for free, and a group of hackers expanded on it to create *NetHack*, which is still being updated today.

**

Craddock: Could you talk more about the atmospheres of the computer labs at MIT and Stanford, and how they influenced the culture you established at Lincoln-Sodbury?

Brian Harvey: There were lots of computer labs at MIT, but most of them were encrusted with rules. There was one dedicated to unofficial student projects, but first-semester freshmen weren't allowed to use it, lest we flunk out. Meanwhile I needed the use of a computer to maintain the mailing list of the student radio station WTBS (now called WMBR), and so someone steered me to the Artificial Intelligence Lab. There I was welcomed and had the run of the place.

When I found a bug in TECO, the text editor we used there, and brought it to one of the "real" system programmers, he told me he was busy and I should fix it myself. He showed me how to find the source files and how to run the assembler, then I was on my own to sink or swim. I couldn't believe they'd let a freshman work on the real system programs. Especially one who'd just walked in the door, with no official status. But that's how it was: there *was* no official status. Months later, Richard Greenblatt, a star programmer who terrified me (not intentionally!), walked over to me, stroked his chin, and said, "I guess we ought to start paying you."

I didn't get to Stanford until several years later, as a graduate student. But there too, there was the official computer center, full of rules, and then there was the AI Lab, complete with a few local high school students who'd just wandered in one day and started working on projects. There was one key that opened all the doors at SAIL [Stanford Artificial Intelligence Library], and everyone had a copy.

So when I found myself at Lincoln-Sudbury Regional High School, I knew I wanted to build that kind of environment: one where kids could wander in and just jump into whatever they wanted to work on, not have to jump through hoops. I didn't arrive with the complete vision of the structure we ended up with, but right away I talked the school into letting me not give grades, since I knew that would ruin the freewheeling atmosphere I wanted.

Craddock: How did you get the position of computer director at the high school?

Brian Harvey: In the early part of my life I was not at all a people person. I was delighted to spend my time dealing with logical, predictable computers. But after a decade of programming, during which I had started reading books about progressive education, one day I suddenly decided I was bored and wanted to become a progressive teacher. My student teaching experiences made it clear to me that I couldn't work in a rigid, traditional school. I was looking for an alternative or "free" school where I could be a math teacher. (Remember, this was before computers took over the world. It never occurred to me that I could be a teacher of computer programming.)

I had a series of job interviews, in which either the school didn't want me or I didn't want the school. While at Stanford, I had gotten to know Paul Goldenberg, who was then working in the MIT Logo group. I had been tell-ing him and his wife, Cindy Carter, how much trouble I was having finding the kind of school where I wanted to work. Luckily, Paul and Cindy were also friends with Larry Davidson, who happened to tell Paul and Cindy how much trouble he was having finding a candidate for a job setting up a computer department at Lincoln-Sudbury (LS). It was Cindy who had the idea of intro-ducing Larry to me.

I was a little dubious about the job, because LS was a regular old school, not a radically progressive one. But it wasn't oppressive, and the school library had several books by Paul Goodman (one of the theorists of progressive education, and a hero of mine), and the vice principal in charge of discipline talked with me at the interview about sociology rather than about demerits and detentions. So the school and I agreed to take a chance on each other.

I was hired as department head and sole member of a new computer depart-ment for two reasons. One is that the math teachers who had set up a computer facility in the math department, Larry Davidson and Phil Lewis, felt that [the computer department] being situated in math might scare off kids who weren't math stars but might still enjoy programming. And the other is that the school was facing layoffs and the rule was last hired first fired within each department. As a newly hired math teacher I would have been gone immediately, but as the sole member of a separate department I was layoff-proof. (I grew up a red diaper baby and a union supporter, so I always felt guilty about that aspect of it.)

Hack, one of the first predecessors to Rogue, and the foundation of NetHack.

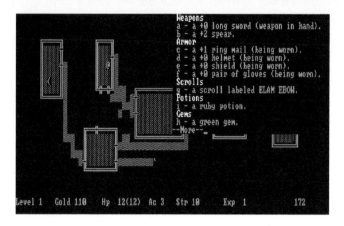

Craddock: Did you encounter much resistance from faculty, administration, and/or parents when you proposed creating an open computer lab where teenagers would be allowed to have (mostly, but not quite totally) free reign over equipment worth thousands of dollars?

Brian Harvey: Surprisingly little. It really matters that computers were rare back then. It's not like now, when everyone sees programming as a survival skill akin to literacy. I'd never get away with it today, but then computer programming was like art or drama, an elective that wasn't going to get anyone into college or keep them out.

The principal of the school was a businessman by training, not an educator. That sounds terrible, but it was actually great, because his strategy was to hire good people and then let them do what they wanted. He originally wanted me to call it the data processing department and teach business applications like computerized bookkeeping, but he knew that it would be better for me to pursue my vision wholeheartedly than to pursue his miserably.

Other teachers had mixed views. Once the computer center was up and running, you'd open the door of the room and hear kids yelling across the room to their friends and project partners, some kids playing games, some just hanging out, and others hard at work with total concentration. Teachers who thought that in a proper classroom every kid is doing the same thing at the same time, quietly, hated it. But other, more progressive teachers loved it. I was amused that every teacher loved or hated it *instantly*, the moment they walked in, without asking questions.

There were a few kids who didn't like the chaotic feeling either, by the way. In a perfect world I would have had two connected rooms with a big window between them, one of which would be designated the quiet room. You could then be in whichever room you wanted, which might change for the same person at different times.

In those early days, there were teachers who didn't understand what computers could do. I once had an English teacher show up in the computer center very upset because the computer had written a kid's English paper. What that turned out to mean was that the kid used a spelling checker! The teacher ended up happy because this primitive spelling checker didn't actually correct the mistakes, but just pointed them out. The kid then had to find out the old-fashioned way how the word should be spelled. On the other hand, there were teachers who embraced the computer as a teaching tool.

My only real enemy at the school was the administrator of the buildings and grounds staff, who was responsible for school security. He managed to go along with the idea of giving kids keys to the room as long as they were for use during hours when the building was open for business. But once kids started wanting to stay all evening, and come in on the weekends, he had to deal with the presence of kids at times when the corridor doors used to be padlocked shut.

Craddock: How were you able to swing getting DEC to pay for 75 percent of the main-frame and a bond to cover the remaining 25 percent?

Brian Harvey: The bond part was just luck. The Massachusetts legislature had just passed a law allowing school boards to issue bonds specifically for computer equipment, and my principal talked the board into using that power.

The DEC grant, though, took a semester of hard work. I wrote the proposal, and we got a sympathetic hearing in part because Sudbury is next door to DEC headquarters in Maynard, and several DEC engineers lived there. But I had many meetings with sales people, technical people, and management people from DEC. (I once almost throttled a kid because he gave me a phone message in the form "someone from DEC called and wants you to call back.")

Of course it helped that I had that decade of programming experience behind me, and a degree from MIT, and experience in particular with DEC products. DEC managers were both skeptical about and intrigued by my ambitious plans, including things like having kids program modifications to the operating system.

What I really wanted was a PDP-10, the machine I'd used at MIT and at Stanford. But I knew they weren't going to give me a half-million-dollar machine, so I asked for a free PDP-11/70, the most powerful model of their minicomputer line. In the end they told me that DEC doesn't like to give 100-percent grants because then people ask for more than they need, but I could have 75 percent off of whatever I wanted.

Craddock: Could you describe the lab? Was it room filled with dumb terminals connected to a mainframe or minicomputer, as seemed to be common in those days?

Brian Harvey: We started with six terminals in the computer center, and additional terminals in the library and some administrative offices where kids and staff shared access. (One of the first ways I put kids to work was running RS-232 cable around the building.) Most of the terminals were VT-100 displays, with a few hardcopy terminals added, mainly because they could display the APL character set, and the displays couldn't. We bought a big line printer too.

The PDP-11 was [kept] in a sort of closet next to the computer center, with a connecting door and a big window. When I first arrived, the school had a much smaller PDP-8 system, with hardcopy terminals connected over 20ma lines rather than RS-232. I don't know if you go back far enough to remember 20ma, but it was very sensitive to static electricity, and the school had done the computer lab the favor of putting it in the only carpeted classroom in the school, so there used to be frequent system crashes.

There were three kids who were official assistant managers of the computer back then, and those kids had keys to the inner sanctum. One time when the computer crashed and none of those kids were around, when I had just arrived at the school and had no idea how to restart the computer, another kid stood right at the door giving me instructions.

Me: Why don't you just come in and do it yourself?

Kid: I'm not allowed in there.

Me: Why on earth not?

Kid: Because of that list of everybody's password stuck to the wall.

Me: That's stupid.

And then I took the list and locked it inside the supply cabinet inside the inner room, and declared that anybody could go into the room. For the first few days, kids were coming and going just for the thrill of it. After a while of that I said anyone could come in, but only if they had a real reason. (We hadn't yet invented the idea of making kids make the rules.)

Also, in the inner room was a couch, for use by the three privileged sysadmin kids. I quickly pulled that out to the big room, so that wouldn't be a reason for anyone to be inside. The inner room had been a de facto clubhouse for the sysadmin kids, but I knew the eventual PDP-11 would take up more space, and I didn't want a lot of traffic in there.

These tiny first steps already established my reputation as an educational radical—nothing about teaching or curriculum, just getting rid of stupid reminders to kids how little their wishes counted at school.

Craddock: I found it interesting that your students went from wanting to hoard software and lock their rivals out of it, to building on the culture you had established by spreading their knowledge far and wide. I know you said you didn't ask or order them to play nicely with others, but I would love to hear more about how the transition happened, from your perspective.

Brian Harvey: Well, I should say first of all that the change was one of degree, not an overwhelming sudden revolution. There were always kids happy to share, and there were always kids more possessive about their work. I give a lot of the credit to one kid in particular, Robert Brown, who quickly became one of the experts on all aspects of programming, and was, from the beginning, eager to share his understanding with others. He never made anyone feel stupid. His ASCII-art graphics library became part of several other kids' games. And as a result, of course, he was extremely well respected by everyone, and a model for other kids' behavior.

When kids were possessive about their programs—and for a while there was a fad of building into game programs a list of who wasn't allowed to play them—I would remind them about all the people who contributed to their work, not only within the LS computer community but also, for example, Ken Thompson and Dennis Ritchie, who wrote the Unix operating system we used, not to mention the taxpayers and the DEC stockholders who paid for the equipment. I didn't tell them what to do, but that doesn't mean I didn't express opinions about how fragile an idea intellectual property is.

It also helped when we started contributing to the Usenix software library. That meant that being communitarian rather than propertarian could get you known in the larger programming community—including, of course, Jay Fenlason's fame for writing *Hack*.

Craddock: Could you go into more detail on the rules and culture of the lab? The kids were allowed to come and go, day or night? (You remind me of my programming teacher in high school, who enforced a similar rule: we could make use of the computer lab as we saw fit, provided we turned in assignments and kept our grades up.)

Brian Harvey: Officially, the kids were turned out by the security guard at 11:00 p.m. Once in a while a kid would hide when the guard came around, and I'd find the kid asleep on the couch in the morning. (This is one respect in which I really didn't understand that the life of a high school kid isn't like the life of an undergraduate for a reason. I'd pulled plenty of all-nighters in computer labs and thought nothing of it when a kid did the same at LS. Many years later I came to understand that that was a sign of something really wrong at the kid's home, calling for adult intervention.)

It helped that we were in a rich community, and it helped that there was no resale value for dumb terminals except to institutions. But even when we got a grant of Atari 800s to use as graphics terminals, none of them went missing. I was and remain very proud of that.

I had read A.S. Neill's *Summerhill* and was in love with the idea of kids making the rules. Our Computer Center Users' Society had weekly meetings that, like the Summerhill General Meeting, were both legislative and judicial. But (as Neill says in the book) it's hard to make self-government work in one classroom when the rest of the school is still adults governing the kids. Our kids weren't nearly as skilled as Summerhill kids at making the meetings work efficiently. Luckily, there were very few serious decisions to be made; the most contentious was who should take precedence when someone is playing games on a terminal and another kid needs it for schoolwork. This was settled with a computerized reservation system.

The kids also organized group social events. We had weekend picnics. The architecture of the room came up once in a while—for example, kids wanted coat hooks, even though of course every kid had a locker, because the lockers were far away from the computer center, and also the kids didn't trust their locked lockers as much as open coat hooks in the computer center.

Peter Blaser organized a chess club and got the school to pay for several plastic chess sets that could be taken out and played on our tables.

As for classes, I started out with an ambitious proposed sequence of courses, but ended up with only two: intro to computers and advanced computer programming. Intro had a sort of curriculum; there was a file cabinet with worksheets on various topics. Intro students had to do a minimal amount of Logo programming—just up to beginning recursion—and a minimal amount of word processing, so they could use the computers for their other schoolwork. After that they could do whatever they wanted, including playing computer games. I made game authors put their names and the school's name in the splash screen, so game players would think, *This was written by a kid just like me*, and be inspired to learn how.

I had gotten permission to offer classes pass/fail, and to pass intro, you had to do the minimal units and not much else. I also invented the variable-unit course, so a kid who took intro out of curiosity and turned out to hate it could complete and pass one unit, then quit, rather than failing two units. I never had as many curriculum worksheets as I wanted; I had hopes for much more than a kid could do in a semester, but as the community grew stronger, writing curriculum gradually felt less and less important to me. Instead what mattered was gathering tools: robot turtles, graphics terminals and printers, programming languages, a Usenet connection.

The kids who took advanced computer programming would start each semester with a proposal for what s/he (overwhelmingly he, alas) would accomplish that semester, and would get the credit for it at the end of the semester. Kids would take it repeatedly, I think less because they needed the units than as an excuse for the time they were spending in the computer lab.

Craddock: You wrote about how the computer lab often look like... well, like a bunch of teenagers had the run of the place. Were you responsible for the lab's upkeep, or did the kids (eventually) straighten up?

Brian Harvey: This is the story of how the Computer Center Users Society was born! The school had custodians who cleaned the classrooms at night, but after a while they refused to work in the computer center because there was *so* much litter. For a while, when it got too terrible, one of us teachers would hit the stop button on the computer and make everyone clean up all the paper. But both the kids and the teachers hated this solution. Meanwhile, my other big pre-CCUS problem was that no matter how early I got to school, there'd be a dozen kids lined up outside the door waiting for me to let them in, and they would never let me go home at night.

It was Larry Davidson who had the brilliant idea of solving these two problems by combining them. Give kids keys to the room if they took on the obligation to keep the room clean. I immediately generalized that to the full *Summerhill* idea of putting kids in charge, period.

We were lucky in that the room had two doors. (This is a Massachusetts fire law for classrooms, but most rooms satisfy the law by having a door that connects to another classroom rather than to the corridor.) So we could leave the standard school lock that teachers have keys to in one of the doors, and put an entirely different lock in the other door.

I was hoping that CCUS members would choose to keep the room clean by cleaning up continually, so the room would always be clean, but instead they chose to set up a system in which one CCUS member each day, in rotation through the membership list, was in charge of cleanup at the end of each school day.

Craddock: I liked your story about password hacking. Could you share others from the LS lab? What anecdotes have stuck with you?

Brian Harvey: Oh, lots. My favorite is about the time I needed some quiet time on the computer to solve a software problem, so I came in one Sunday at 10:00 a.m.—and couldn't get a terminal because they were all in use! But what makes this a funny story is that just as I walked in the door, one kid was saying to another kid, "I hate school." That was the only time I ever literally rolled on the floor laughing. (To which the kid said "This isn't school; this is the computer center.")

Another great moment won't seem so funny to you because it's one of those you-had-to-be-there stories, but I'll try: Kid A (male) and B (female) are sitting on the couch necking with great enthusiasm. Surrounding them are a cloud of other kids arguing vociferously about whether it's okay for A and B to behave that way in the computer center. Both sides of the argument had several adherents. I love those situations; the kids feel the weight of being in charge much more than when it's something obvious like cleanup.

Meanwhile, in the opposite corner of the room, C, who is the most clean-cut, proper, polite, dignified kid in the group, is teaching D, a freshman, how to play *Breakout*. Back at the argument, there's one of those moments when, for a second, nobody is talking. Just then, C says to D, "…and what you have to do is penetrate deeper." Everyone cracks up, and of course C makes it even funnier by saying "What? What'd I say?"

One time I pulled an all-nighter solving a system bug, and when kids started coming in in the morning, Jonathan [Payne] decided he was going to be me for the morning so I could rest. So the kids who would ordinarily have been calling "Brian! Brian!" to get me to come debug their programs were instead calling "Jonathan! Jonathan!" and at one point he did that cartoon thing of trying to walk in three directions at once. (Everyone got into this, and I think there were actually more requests for help than there would have been on a normal day.)

Craddock: What can you tell me about Jay Fenlason, Kenny Woodland, Mike Thome, and Jonathan Payne? What grades were they in when you met, and what kind of students were they? Were they excited by the possibilities offered to them by computers?

Brian Harvey: That last question is funny; they all *lived* in the computer center. I don't really understand how any of the computer gang managed to pass their other classes. Most of them I met as freshmen, although some of them were still in junior high (this was before the invention of "middle school") when they started hanging out in the computer center after school hours.

[Digression for funny story. Every year the math teachers at LS had a joint meeting with the junior high math teachers to make sure they were all on the same page about what the high school teachers could expect kids to have learned in junior high. At one of these meetings, the teacher at Curtis Junior High who ran their school computer [lab] commented that kids didn't seem so interested in computers anymore; he used to have a bunch of kids hanging out after school but didn't any more. We had to explain to him where his kids were now.]

Jonathan was an exception. He spent his first two years hanging out at the library (and trying to get other kids in trouble by pulling the little magnetic strip off a library book and stashing it in someone's backpack). But we had terminals installed at the library, and you could play games on them, and—as I said earlier—the games made it clear that they were written by kids, and so late sophomore year he appeared in the computer center. But he very quickly became one of the leading experts; his big claim to fame was JOVE, an Emacs-subset editor for small computers.

Mike was much less bouncy than most of the kids. He liked to climb up to a little ledge at the top of one of the walls and sit there cross-legged reading. Don't misunderstand; he wasn't autistic or anything; he was very much part of the social group. He was just more able to sit in one place and not be in the heat of every ephemeral activity. So he became sort of the stereotype wise man of the group. Everyone looked up to him—me, too!—because he never yelled; he just always did the right thing calmly.

Exploring one of *Hack's* procedurally generated dungeons on MS-DOS.

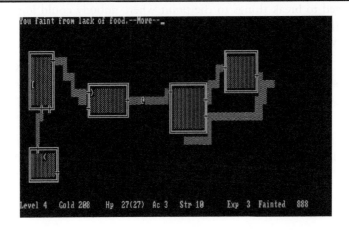

Craddock: I understand those boys created *Hack* in 1982, while at Lincoln-Sodbury. Did you follow *Hack's* development? If so, in what way? Did you encourage or contribute to it?

Brian Harvey: Really, Jay created *Hack*. Other kids contributed little bits. If you see names other than Jay's in the credits, it's because Jay really took in the lesson about not being possessive about one's creations. He did it because he wanted to improve *Rogue*, but—very unusually in those days—*Rogue* was distributed without source code.

I was certainly aware of *Hack*—I was their teacher, and I mostly knew about everyone's projects. I encouraged Jay as I encouraged everyone, but I didn't have any special feeling pro or con that particular project, if that's what you're asking. I'm sure Jay asked me questions as he was working, as everyone did, but I don't remember any particular way in which I contributed.

Craddock: What led you to leave LS in 1982?

Brian Harvey: Ach—this is a hard question for me to answer. With the benefit of hindsight, I think the deep answer is that it was my first teaching job, I was very, very invested in it, I loved the kids, and therefore I took it personally when kids messed up. I wasn't yet a parent, and I guess I had an overly simplistic view about what teenagers are like, or what they could be like when put in charge of their own lives.

The surface answer is about password hacking. As I've written and you've read, the first time (that I know about) when a kid wanted to write a login simulator, I smiled benignly, thinking that that would be a minor activity. I myself grew up at the MIT AI Lab, where, back then, there was no such thing as passwords. I was certainly a hacker, in the original sense: I wanted to know how everything worked. But I had no curiosity about other people's secrets. So I underestimated how much energy the LS kids would put into password hacking.

Over time I got more and more annoyed about it. At one point I modified our system so that turning off echoing required special privileges. And then finally, one day when I had the day off, I was called in because three kids had independently made efforts to crack the system and two of them had managed to break things to the point where nobody could log in. I was furious. (That evening my mom called me up, I said "*Hello?*" and she immediately said "What's the matter?" because she could hear it in my voice.)

That was, I think, in 1980–1981. And that's when I decided I was leaving. It took me another year to do it, because I had to hire and train my replacement. None of the candidates who applied had both the technical expertise and the progressive spirit we needed. In the end I twisted the arm of Paul Goldenberg, who'd been pivotal in getting me to LS in the first place, to take the job. But 1981–1982 was an unhappy time for me, and therefore for the kids too; I got angry a lot.

Craddock: What led to you and the *Hack* crew staying in touch?

Brian Harvey: There's nothing special about *Hack* in this respect; I'm in touch with dozens of LS computer kids. This was probably the most intense time of my life. I felt part of a family, in a way I've never felt before or since. My best friends in the world are mostly LS teachers and kids. Former kids. Today is Jonathan's 50th birthday. Makes me feel antique. I'm even friends with some of the kids' kids!

Craddock: Andries Brouwer, who built on top of *Hack*, told me he got *Hack* from "the Lincoln-Sodbury tape," which I took to mean tapes containing code from programs were passed around. He hasn't clarified, so I thought I'd ask you on the off-chance you know: did LS make a habit of saving code on tapes and passing them around to other institutions?

Brian Harvey: I think what he means is "from the LS contribution to the Usenix tape." Usenix is the Unix users' group, and they used to distribute contributed software periodically.

14

Super Marketing Showdown
InFamous *versus* Prototype

InFamous and *Prototype* were two of my favorite games during the Xbox 360/PS3 generation of consoles. They were beautiful to behold, rooted in moral choices, and gave readers near-total autonomy in the fantasy of playing a superhero—or a supervillain.

But what set both games apart was their close proximity to one another. Through total coincidence, two developers—Radical Entertainment and Sucker Punch Productions—were working on two very similar games. Eerily similar. Inevitably, their release dates fell close enough together that many consumers felt forced to choose between one or the other.

Expanding on my interest in marketing for games, I spoke with Sucker Punch head Nate Fox about the development of and marketing for *InFamous*. Next, Chris Ansell weighs in on subjects such as the pros and cons of developing a game similar to a competitor's. Finally, Lindsey Williamson Christy, *Prototype's* senior development director, shares how two divisions worked together to achieve the same goal: Launch a successful product.

**

Craddock:	Today, most consumers know Sucker Punch as the *InFamous* company. Take me back to pre-electrical superpowers. What interested you and the team in making a game about superheroes and morality?
Nate Fox:	We got done with the *Sly Cooper* franchise, and we wanted to do something more realistic. We saw where the market was heading. At the time, *Grand Theft Auto III* was super popular. It kind of redefined people's expectations of what a video game [could be]. I remember playing *GTA* and thinking, *Man, I wish I could fly.*
	So, there you go. *Sly Cooper* had a lot of the same moves as Cole MacGrath: a lot of climbing and jumping. That works really well in a video game because it's very physically expressive, so we made a superhero game.
Craddock:	I love the *InFamous* series for many reasons, but one is the movement. It's so fluid and seamless. You could call it Parkour: The Video game.

Nate Fox: That's really nice of you to say. That was a big conversation point, as you might imagine. People had a hard time picturing an open-world game without a car, but it seemed like the right thing to do. It honors the [comic book] subject matter. When you think about *Spider-Man*, his form of locomotion is so key.

And it's not like we were the first to do an open-world superhero game. *Spider-Man 2* on PS2 was amazing, with really amazing locomotion. Another one was [*The Incredible*] *Hulk: Ultimate Destruction*, which was actually the game that came out before Prototype that the same team worked on. It was awesome. The Hulk had this great jump mechanic, and he could run up walls and weaponize things in the environment, like ripping up cars and turning them into gauntlets.

Craddock: Was the fact that you were building your own world rather than working within the boundaries of a licensed IP, like *Batman* or *Spider-Man*, helpful in deciding what your character could do?

Nate Fox: That was really handy. When you're making a video game, you're looking for things that work well inside of a game space. Aiming and shooting work well; jumping and climbing work well. I can only imagine how much pain people who have to adapt existing franchises [to a video game] have to go through.

For example, if you're making a *Wolverine* game, the expectation is you can cut through anything. But how do you make a video game level with limits for a guy who can cut through anything? You can't honor the core fantasy of being *Wolverine* because of what video games are capable of doing.

I think flying is another example. It's really no fun to fly in games, or at least it's not often very fun. Even though it's great in movies, it doesn't really work out in games. It's really challenging. We were really excited to be able to make our own superhero. We felt very lucky to have that opportunity. When we went on to *InFamous: Second Son*, we said, "Look, the most fun thing about any superhero is their origin story," so we felt, "Let's just do it again."

Sucker Punch's *InFamous*.

Craddock:	Sony was firmly behind *InFamous*, one of the advantages of developing a game for a specific platform, I'd imagine. What was the collaboration between Sucker Punch and Sony on marketing?
Nate Fox:	Sony has a marketing department, and we collaborated with them on the message. They see early builds of the game, and they see pitches, and they say "Oh, okay, the game's going to be like this?" They have to project forward in their mind's eye of what it's going to be, because what they're looking at [at that stage] is very crude geometry. We showed them what we had, and inevitably, games are going to change during development.

Whatever direction your plan goes in, it won't be what you ship with because you're following the fun. Sony's marketing department knows that. What they offer that's really unique is, they say, "Of all the things you've shown us, the thing that lights up our eyes is this." And they kind of underline it. That's when you know a feature you're working on has widespread appeal or impact.

Usually we try and double down on things that we see other people, particularly people outside of the studio who have a fresh perspective, get excited about. Marketers are usually the first people to do that.

Craddock:	What I find interesting about the Sucker Punch/Sony relationship is that both studios had a vested interest in the property. For Sucker Punch, you're building your own IP. For Sony, they're paying a lot of money for that IP. Given that, I'd imagine you occasionally had differences of opinion regarding what aspects of the game to feature in marketing. What did Sony want to zero in on?
Nate Fox:	Karma. In the *InFamous* games, you're an everyday person who gets super powers, and you get to choose them for good or evil. That split, where you get to choose how to use your powers, really was supported by some early feedback from marketing people. We were originally thinking about the game as sort of more of a sim, where there are different social levels and needs, and we would chart these around the city in *InFamous*.

It kind of boiled down to treating people well or treating people poorly. Because of the genre we were in, where there are these really strong lines between heroes and villains, it seemed like we should go farther in that direction and make [the delineation] clearer. The marketing people said, "You should make this a huge part of the game and leverage it." I think they had great vision.

Craddock:	I have to think marketing a game centered on morality, or karma, in this case, is difficult because that marketing seems to promise huge choices with huge consequences. How do you design choices that people care about, versus ones that feel shallow and game-y?
Nate Fox:	To be honest, that's something we struggled with a good deal. Originally, all of the choices were very morally gray. Like, do you take food for yourself or give food to people who need it equally as much? I thought that was really cool. You want to put that sort of dilemma in a video game, but it was really tough. People got frustrated because they wanted to role play as a hero or a villain, and it was not clear to them how to do it, so they got angry. They wanted to be one or the other.

We had to end up sign-posting the choices a little bit more. That [save girl-friend or strangers] one is one of the rare choices where it's not a good-or-evil thing. Our original intention was to make [choices] that were more gray, but we got continuous feedback that they ultimately caused more harm than good to people's experience in the game.

Craddock: I always play as a hero in these types of games because I feel bad about doing bad things. Is designing "good" choices difficult?

Nate Fox: It's certainly more challenging to play *InFamous* as a good person because the world is filled with pedestrians who are kind of the studio audience to your actions. They're all around you, and a stray shot from you can hurt them, and the game pays attention to you hurting innocent bystanders. It's no joke that being a hero is harder.

However, we tried to offset that by giving you extra powers of precision: more sniper-like skills versus shotgun-style skills where you're just spraying and praying.

Craddock: Once marketing was ready, how did the campaign play out?

Nate Fox: There were two ad campaigns that I remember for *InFamous*. One was about a comic book coming to life. We would go from graphic [novel] panels to 3D action. In the game, we did have 2D movies that looked like comic books with motion. We were totally inspired by graphic novels to make the game, more so than movies, really. That was a way to tell people, "If you like graphic novels, you will like this game." It was the 2D movies that we produced that started people in the marketing department down that road of thought.

The other marketing angle that I think caught the most heat was a video made by Sony San Diego. They have a marketing group, and they made this video called The Beauty of Powers. It was just the hero using his powers in slow motion in the world, doing these extraordinarily cool things. Everybody in the office, we didn't produce this movie; we just watched it. And when we watched it we thought, *Oh my God. That's our game?* And it's totally our game, it's just that when you slow down time to see all the detail and see just how expressive the hero can be, man, the game just looks awesome.

We'd just got so used to playing it as twitch speed. We didn't understand how cool it was to have these powers, and how balletic the hero could be. That changed our mind. When we saw that video, we said, "We need to make a game that's equal to this video." That's another example of the marketing department affecting the choices we made in the development of the game.

Craddock: Consumers ended up having to make a different sort of choice, because *Prototype* and *InFamous* were being promoted around the same time.

Nate Fox: I can't tell you the first time I saw *Prototype*. It must have been on the Internet. The moment that made me scared was when I played it at the New York Comic Con, and it was so polished. It was their introductory level where the hero can run around and whale on tanks. It was beautiful, and the animations and effects were really good.

Craddock: I can't think of that situation happening very often.

Nate Fox:	There are only two other examples of this that I can think of. Maybe my memory's not very good, but they're both in film: *Dante's Peak*, and some other volcano movie that came out around the same time; and then *Deep Impact*, and *Armageddon*. They were both about meteors going deep into the earth. Both of those pairs of films had the exact same issue where through random circumstance, they were coming out around the same time and were pretty hard to tell apart for viewers.
	There should be a name for this. It is pretty interesting time when it happens because it seems to be a rare thing. You strive so hard to have definition in whatever art form you're working on, and then to see all of your supposed creative choices being replicated by another team shows you that it's not so much what you're choosing as much as it is the spirit of the time. You're just surfing the zeitgeist.
Craddock:	As much as consumers probably want to buy every game out there, sometimes we only have $60 and have to choose between two games that look similar. Were you aware of *Prototype*?
Nate Fox:	I remember doing work for the *Game Informer* cover. That was a huge deal for us; we were super excited about that. It made everybody feel excited and like we could pull it off. Then I remember watching *Prototype* on this [show] called *X Play*. They were interviewing the devs, and the devs were showing all these moves that the hero could do, and how smooth he looked running up walls and jumping.
	It was scary. It looked so good, better than what we had. We were on an emotional seesaw of us showing a feature, then they would show a feature, back and forth. But from a marketing perspective it felt like [we] were pretty independent of *Prototype*. We definitely wanted to get out before *Prototype*, but we had no idea when they were shipping. It was just a crap shoot. I can only assume it didn't really help.
	Say for instance that you've played an awesome game like *Mass Effect*. Then a game that's similar to *Mass Effect* comes out over the next couple of weeks. You're less apt to have enthusiasm for another *Mass Effect*. However, it is an awesome game, and if a game like it comes out three months later, after you've had time to finish it and had time to play something [different], then it would have been ideal.
	I do wish there would have been a little bit more time between the releases of our products. Then I think we would have helped each other immensely regardless of how came out first or second.
Craddock:	Besides being scary, can competing—explicitly or otherwise—with a similar game have advantages?
Nate Fox:	In retrospect, I'm really glad *Prototype* came out when it did because it pushed us to make a better game. I mean, we always want to make a great game, but the terror we felt because of *Prototype* looming pushed us even farther, and gamers win when that happens. I was glad for that sense of very direct competition because I think both games were improved by it.

Gamers probably bought both. If you like *Prototype*, you're probably going to like *InFamous*, and vice versa. I'd never thought of that, but yeah, that makes sense. From a marketing standpoint that's not a bad angle. It's almost like there were three press stories: there was coverage of *InFamous*; there was coverage of *Prototype*; and then there was coverage of the fact that these two games were being made in isolation, yet on such parallel tracks.

Craddock:	One piece of marketing people remember is Sucker Punch's interactions with Ben "Yahtzee" Croshaw, a game critic. How did that get started?
Nate Fox:	Yahtzee had started some kind of illustration feud where he was asking for pictures of both heroes riding unicorns and wearing tutus or something like that, and we exchanged art. The coolest thing about that—I'll be totally honest—is that Yahtzee knew who we were.

It's weird to have somebody who you watch every week aware of the game you're working on. Yahtzee had a ton of influence on our studio. I think it was every Wednesday morning he would publish, and we would all watch.

Radical Entertainment's *Prototype*.

Craddock:	I've always wondered if developers from one team keep an eye on how a similar type of game is shaping up, and second-guess their choices when they see what the other studio is doing. Was that ever the case with *InFamous*, or did you all just stay focused on your product?
Nate Fox:	To be honest, no, we did not make any choices about what was in the game or not in the game based on *Prototype*. We just kept talking about what would

be best for our core vision of our game, which was, "everyday guy gets super powers and decides whether to use them for good or evil."

Frankly, we would have just followed the fun with powers. You don't have a very complete picture of what another person's game is just from a trailer or small, playable demo, but when I did end up playing their demo, it was nice to see that their game was more of a brawler while ours was more of a ranged game. That might seem a small difference between the game, but to me it was a sigh of relief: we really weren't in the same interactive experience base.

All video games stand on the shoulders of other video games. I don't know where a video game's soul begins or ends, but I do know it's a good idea to have a couple of core fantasies you're trying to deliver. We really tried to make that work [fluid movement] work, and we were very much inspired by the *Tony Hawk* games because they had a sense of flow to them. We knew, in trying to create this momentum-based flow gameplay that was akin to *Tony Hawk*, what we were targeting from an emotional experience perspective.

You just hold to that. You don't add things because you can. If you do that, you can get lost and muddied. But that's not really soul; that's just making decisions that lead to the same place to see if we could get as far as possible in that direction. For right or wrong, you have to follow that direction.

Craddock: Did you know anyone from Radical who was working on *Prototype*?

Nate Fox: During the development of *InFamous*, I didn't know anyone at Radical. Since that studio closed its doors, we actually have hired a couple of people from Radical, so I've been able to talk to them now since we're on the same team. From what they've said, it sounded like they had the same kind of nervousness around a competing product, and also the value of both of us trying to do better because of the other product.

Craddock: Comparisons between *Prototype* and *InFamous* seemed inevitable, both back then and in retrospect, because both games were bound to have some similarities given the superhero genre in which they worked. Movement, for example, was very fun and somewhat similar.

Nate Fox: That's one thing that I think both the *Prototype* [team] and we clearly both did: We watched those teenagers in Russia post their videos doing amazing parkour moves in old industrial sites, and we tried to put that feeling in the game, that kind of rebellious, physical mastery of urban landscapes. Parkour, man. That was from the early aughts.

Craddock: The fact that *InFamous* was a PS3 exclusive whereas *Prototype* would be on both consoles was an obvious point to mention in marketing. Did you consider it a boon?

Nate Fox: Sony is certainly an outstanding partner to us. They're very supportive, but during the PS3 era, Xbox 360 was the dominant platform, so I assumed that if you were going to buy a copy of *Prototype*, you were going to do it on the 360. But if you were going to buy *InFamous*, you had to get it on PS3. The people who bought *Prototype* on PS3 probably did it because they didn't have an Xbox 360.

I love all of the PlayStation exclusives. They keep coming, and I totally believe that is a testament to Sony corporate: just backing up studios and letting them explore and make things. That game *The Last of Us*—on paper, who thinks, *Oh, we need another zombie game.* But they just let Naughty Dog follow their passion, and it's a masterpiece. People all over the world have richer lives because of it.

I don't see a lot of other publishers doing that. Because Sony does it as first-party exclusives, that makes their consoles all the more valuable to us as gamers because it's the only place you can experience games like *God of War*.

Craddock:	Was the rollout of the campaign Sucker Punch's decision, or Sony's?
Nate Fox:	There was our debut at E3. I think the fellow who ran Sony at the time, Phil Harrison, described the game as one where you got to choose if you are going to be good or evil. That was a feature that we hadn't really, totally decided we were going to do. But after he said it to the E3 public, we were very committed. [laughs]

We had a very good idea, but we didn't know how we were going to handle it. We just knew we were going to figure out how to handle it after that [announcement]. The Beauty of Powers video was by far the most impactful. Even working on *InFamous 2*, we would watch that video and think, *How can we live up to this thing?*

Craddock:	Chris, we've talked about how you got started at SCEE. Let's move forward a bit, and walk your path to Radical.
Chris Ansell:	I was working in Singapore for Blizzard Asia Pacific. This was after I'd worked in Europe with Sony, and then I'd done Asia for four years, Pan-Asia marketing for *World of WarCraft*. I was very excited to tackle North America, get that added to the bow and see what life was like over there. I had the opportunity to do an internal transfer with our then-parent company, Vivendi, which owned a bunch of game companies including Blizzard and Radical for a time. I was lucky enough to get invited over to Radical and to set up marketing from within the studio.
Craddock:	So the team had established a marketing department?
Chris Ansell:	They hadn't really had [marketing] yet. They were very keen to improve the quality of marketing that was happening to their games, to keep it accountable to the schedules that game development and producing have. And, I think, to ensure better camaraderie with teams—to have teams energized by marketing and not annoyed by it. Also to kind of make sure that the marketing message— the language we use with consumers, the visuals, video footage, everything— was simpatico with the devs, the creative minds behind the game.

Often, if you separate marketing from developers, you get different visions. I'm a strong believer that every voice should be heard, and marketing should reflect a game's strengths. Game developers live and breathe [their games] every minute of every day, so why would you not take the chance to feed off that energy and their ideas, and translate that into a strong consumer message? That was a big appeal.

Craddock: How were you feeling about being sort of the vanguard of a marketing team for a company like Radical?

Chris Ansell: I landed in Vancouver. The first six months, I remember almost wanting to vomit in the morning while I was brushing my teeth because I was so intimidated by how much talent there was at the studio. I felt like until I could get some runs on the board as a marketing guy, just being surrounded by these genius programmers and concept artists was like, "Am I worthy?"

It was nice getting through that, and they're so supportive. Vancouver culture is very warm, family oriented, and human, which I've come to appreciate sense. I came across and we started building up relations with the publisher and developing our marketing capacity in-house.

Craddock: How soon after starting the job did you dig into *Prototype*?

Chris Ansell: When I joined Radical, I think on the first day, the CEO took me around to all the executive producers. They had four projects on the go at that time. They had 420 people at Radical, which was its peak. There were four projects, and I'd be working on all four of them. They were at different stages, and I remember the one I was most excited about, because it spoke to me, was just this series of animation tests.

It showed particular sequences of what powers this character, Alex Mercer, would have: spikes coming out of his back, his arm transforming into a blade, all the physics, the crowd sizes. It was really high-tech stuff.

That was the first time I kind of had an inkling of the scope of the game, and it just seemed so cool. I really fell in love with the concept, and it just kind of became our baby over the next six or seven years.

Exploring and fighting *in InFamous.*

Craddock: What were your priorities for marketing the game at that early stage?

Chris Ansell: I think priority one was establishing a really enigmatic, core character that we knew gamers would want to be, or sort of aspire to even in terms of his look. This was the start of the hoodie era. [laughs] We'd been announced around the same time as *Assassin's Creed*, and they had this white hoodie.

We had a unique vision for making [*Prototype*] very on-the-street. You were an everyman: As long as you had a hoodie, you could be Alex Mercer. The guys, Eric Holmes and Dennis Deitweiler and the artists, did a great job. It was their baby, creating a backstory and lore around Alex Mercer and his motivations, as well as the world around him. So it was important, I think, to first get the right look for the character. We went through a lot of iterations for the look, right up until late in [development]. His jackets and clothing were changing pretty regularly, so we had to settle on a final look.

To create a salable, iconic character, we really wanted to hammer on the whole gray lines. There was no good or bad in this world. Obviously he does extremely violent things. We wanted to paint the character with an air of mystery so the player could inject morality into the character: you can play him how you like. We hadn't really seen many anti-heroes in games. It wasn't a popular thing yet, so we really played up that angle in the press. There was a lot of attention given to that, a lot of interest, because people were like, "What's that mean?"

And then the scope of the open world. The open world is kind of the second [main] character in any open-world game. We made sure to release a lot of videos, screenshots, examples of great physics. We were super proud of our massive crowds. I think we had the best tech at the time for pushing incredible volumes of crowds and density on PlayStation 3.

At early behind-the-scenes demos at Gamescom and GDC, we'd have a full roster. Some of my fondest memories in the industry were watching journalists who were often very tired—they come in the afternoon looking like, "All right, what's this about?" with their shoulders slouched because they're exhausted—and as we would move through this demo, which escalated in terms of the action of the screen and what Alex could do, all the beasts chasing you over skyscrapers. It was so fun to watch them slowly reach down for their pens, slowly open their backpacks and grab their notebooks, leaning forward with their eyes wide. That was very rewarding.

Craddock: The thing about *Prototype* that caught my eye right away was how impressive it looked, both screenshots and in motion.

Chris Ansell: We knew we had an incredibly accomplished engine. That was done in-house. So it was about pushing the character, selling our unique anti-hero, and promoting the open world as a second character.

I think the third thing was showing examples of the calamitous physics interactions and systems interactions, which is always super fun: bringing down helicopters that crash into something else, which causes the crowds to run. All of those happy accidents are emergent gameplay, which was the third tier.

Craddock: What is the process of marketing a game at a trade show like E3, with so much noise and so many other games stealing attendees' attention?

Chris Ansell: I've always believed that the small things you do in life result in the biggest impacts. You hold a door open for a person before a job interview, and that person ends up being the CEO. I take the same approach with games marketing. Not only is it important to be excited and enthusiastic for the smallest news blogger whom you've never heard of all the way up to the IGNs of the world—if you continue doing that, the puzzle pieces will connect for anyone looking to market a product. Everyone knows someone through first-, second-, third-degree separations.

That small-time blogger might then recommend [your game] to a friend who's just become editor-in-chief of a major publication. It's very important to treat everyone with energy, excitement, and respect.

Craddock: That was for outside Radical. What about internally? How did you communicate the project vision to publishers and other executives?

Chris Ansell: This was a huge focus for us at Radical. We had just been bought by Activision, so we were kind of thinking, *Well, who is Radical? Now [Activision] has* Guitar Hero, *they have* Call of Duty. We were fighting for internal attention with sales managers. You want to make sure you're putting your best foot forward within the organization, and that those people are thinking as much about your game as they are the big titles.

We launched a very aggressive internal marketing campaign. We put top regional office people's names into our posters and mailing it to them. They were so proud to get them and hung them up over their desks. We had our posters customized with our best internal contacts and hanging in people's offices, highly visible.

That was part of it: give your team the assets they need to help them sell, and feel super proud and accomplished by having these amazing assets they're proud to show off to retailers. If you're the first to get there and arm them with those tools, you'll win. We used to say, "If you're excellent and you're early, you'll win."

Craddock: Was there any overlap in marketing strategies for consumers versus internal parties?

Chris Ansell: I think they're pretty much identical. I like to think about what appeals to the inner young gamer in all of us. What's that elemental appeal factor? Then I go straight for that. Don't bother so much with the technicalities of our [professional] titles.

If something really excites the dev team and me—because everyone is very critical of their own work—if we think something is good or very good, I knew the public would think it was unbelievably awesome. I also think of our staff as part of the public. I'd use the dev team as a litmus test for assets, for copyrighting, get them to suggest their own tag lines and phrases.

The gold is in the goldmine. By working with the development team, I got to work in the goldmine.

Craddock: There was, of course, another superhero-themed game in development along-side *Prototype*. That was Sucker Punch's *InFamous*. When did you become aware of *InFamous*, and what were your thoughts as someone in charge of promoting a competing product?

Chris Ansell: I think their announcement trailer was when we first heard about it. There might have been screenshots before that, but definitely when we saw the announcement trailer we said, "Oh, it's very similar." They only had a teaser trailer; that was the only asset they released for a very long time. We certainly had the opportunity with the first *Prototype* to jump ahead of them with the amount of assets we were releasing.

We had a lot of asset-generating power and autonomy, with the marketing team being in the studio. It felt like maybe the guys at Sucker Punch didn't have that, and they had to maybe work through official systems, and that maybe slowed down the rate at which they could release assets. We took advantage of that and tried to steal the march by talking more, showing more, involving the community—which now is [essential]—but even then we were keen to show work-in-progress stuff and involve the community as much as possible. We knew how important it was to bring them in.

Craddock: *Prototype* and *InFamous* were similar, yes, but they had unique strengths. What did you perceive as *Prototype*'s strengths, and how did you play to them in marketing?

Chris Ansell: I've always tried to carve my own path with a product and not let other people's products dictate my planning. That tends to water down—I call it "oatmeal"—it tends to oatmeal down your message into this slimy, generic mush that's forgettable. You do want to find where your edges poke out by finding out what pricks people's ears up, their attention, and hammer in those directions so you stand out because things on edges tend to get noticed.

We were keen to push what we knew was great and unique about our game. It was over-the-top violent and had these calamitous, happy accidents. The open-world scale, the speed, the density of crowds, the cool anti-hero character. I think Sucker Punch had generally more of a good-guy character. It might have helped in terms of reaffirming where we were different and we kept pushing in [our] direction.

We knew that generally people—especially teens early-20s gamers—everybody wants to do a bit of rebellion in their video games. Look at *GTA*. So we played very much to that. We played it very close to the line with some of the graphic violence. Anything that gave a feeling of escape and a power fantasy—even if it was about doing pretty nasty things—we definitely wanted to play that up. Obviously it's a video game with simplistic graphics compared to a film, but we were keen to show the ultimate power you could unleash in this incredible sandbox, and play to the Mature rating rather than being afraid of it.

Sucker Punch had their thing, but I do think we had a massive range of powers. [*Prototype*] was almost like a fighting game, and we wanted to show that breadth of ability. I think Sucker Punch had, specifically, electrical powers.

The game looked gorgeous and was fantastic, but we wanted to keep playing to our strength: that grittier, darker tone. We had vehicles that were completely controllable, like tanks and airplanes, with all the freedom of motion they allowed.

Craddock: Sucker Punch had the advantage of Sony putting their weight behind *InFamous* because it was being developed exclusively for Sony hardware. What partners did Radical work with to design *Prototype*'s advertising?

Chris Ansell: We spent time investing in great partners to help build the IP up pretty early. We worked with Dark Horse to create a *Prototype* comic that established the *Prototype* backstory. We worked with NECA to develop action figures for the game. We almost had one of the world's biggest music artists play the main character. I won't go too much into that, but it was interesting and would have been kind of cool.

Craddock: A big part of superheroes is their powers. How did you promote the sorts of wild and crazy things players would be able to do?

Chris Ansell: The guys packed so many powers and unique abilities into Alex. We did a lot of mini videos, like story modules, showing all the ways you could interact with friend and foe. There was a wide variety of combos. We were big fighting-game fans so we had a lot of combo attacks and the strategy of one-versus-one and one-versus-many melee combat. If I remember, *InFamous* was more ranged, while we were generally about melee. We also had weapons you could pick up: like rocket launchers.

Craddock: I also couldn't help comparing and contrasting, as a consumer intrigued by both games, their styles of movement. *InFamous* doesn't let you fly, but you can glide, climb, all that stuff. *Prototype*'s protagonist seems to have even more movement options.

Chris Ansell: A huge thing was flying, the gliding and flying. People just loved it. We'd just come off of [*The Incredible*] *Hulk: Ultimate Destruction*, one of the world's most highly rated and beloved superhero games. Eric Holmes, the designer, also designed *Prototype*, so we took a lot of [*Ultimate Destruction*'s] freedom of movement, that feeling of power. *Prototype* is like a flying fantasy game, and that worked beautifully.

The speed of action combined with our locomotion was great. There were amazing moments just from playing the game. For example, two trucks would collide. They'd be tumbling in midair, and if you hit jump at the right time, because of the way the locomotion worked with the AI, you'd see Alex, in midair, land on the spinning trucks, run over one surface as they spin, then do a flip onto the next one and then get to a building. It was like, "Wow, did you see that?" There were so many happy accidents thanks to our tech base. The game just gave us endless little moments that we could capture and share with the community.

In one of our earliest announcements, we did an intentional leak of five short video clips. I think they're still on GameTrailers. They got a huge reaction. It's always fun to do the, "Oops! We may have leaked this… but we may not have" tactic with press. It's great.

Craddock: One thing I remember from back then was when I would think of *Prototype* or *InFamous*, I'd automatically associate it with the other game. What do you think was responsible for that mental linking?

Chris Ansell: For as long as I've been in the industry, there's a weird zeitgeist effect: As soon as someone comes up with an innovative idea and you can see it in a teaser trailer—my goodness, how often do you see one or two other people who [present] the same idea at the same time? I think we live in a Petri dish of influences in the west.

It happens a lot, so there wasn't a huge concern. I think it's good to have a competitor who keeps you honest, and it gets [both teams] that much more fired up to prove themselves and win that battle. I was eager to approach the marketing campaign, especially in light of *InFamous* [appearing similar], such that no one would ever mention *InFamous* on a forum or a YouTube comment without people organically wanting to bring *Prototype* into the conversation. I wanted to set up that fun rivalry.

Craddock: Were you interested in playing to that mental association?

Chris Ansell: We didn't have to do much consciously. In official social media responses, we always acknowledged and were complimentary to competitors. We had a lot of questions from press at the time. I think it was actually more the press who were looking for the comparisons and keen to get both our opinions. They wanted to explore it further and we were happy to oblige, while sort of painting why we thought we had a very original and clear differentiation.

Also, it's very easy and comfortable for all of us to pattern match—to kind of feel like you're in control and know exactly what something is by immediately thinking of a light product. You can say, "Oh, it's just like this, but with this." It's just a comfortable thing that we do as gamers. *Prototype* certainly had a lot of that. You'd see it a lot on the forums, even today. *Battleborn* really suffered from that: you kind of instantly get this comparison, and it's tough to shake because it comes from a grassroots level.

So I think it was more consumers and press who were making that association, and we were happy to continue explaining the differentiation, but not be overly combative about it. If we could get more people into open-world [games], awesome. It was good for both teams. The worst thing you want in marketing is to not ever be talked about.

That's way worse than the potential for a negative conversation or a strained conversation. To be invisible is guaranteed death, whereas if you've been talked about, you're at least giving people a chance to learn more and make up their own minds. Maybe they fall in love with it and become a big influencer, but not being talked about is death.

Craddock: As we've discussed, *InFamous* was exclusive to PS3, while *Prototype* was multiplatform. That automatically stirred up "console war" discussions, particularly on the *InFamous* side, where devout PS3 owners wanted to prop up "their" game. Did you see that as a good thing? Was it something you could use?

Chris Ansell: There's always a proxy. I think consoles have been great for that. I did it as a kid, and I think every generation of kids with their console wars has done it. One of the things that I've done with previous titles, with *Prototype*, is there's so much natural and kinetic energy in the console war. Teens, 20-year-olds, 30-year-olds and above, arguing why their console is better than the competitor's. We've tried in the past to insert our product, and stand it on top of that existing fight.

It's fantastic from an awareness point of view if someone can't mention PlayStation or Xbox without also mentioning the title you're promoting as an example. We were certainly having a lot of fun, and I'm sure the guys at Sucker Punch were, when we did the *Prototype* versus *InFamous* campaign, because it was impossible for any Sony fan to mention *InFamous* without [also] talking about *Prototype* and vice versa.

We kind of leaped into that existing, back-and-forth, competitive energy. That's certainly a strategy: inserting your product into an existing conversation.

We had an internally developed engine, a very high-tech engine. We were able to develop it equally for both formats all the way through. Often I think gamers will assume, "Oh, you're favoring one [platform] over the other and one's going to be subpar." We didn't have any of those problems at Radical because we were always a multi-format company. Our technology always supported [multiple platforms] at the same time. We were keen to show gameplay on both machines, and to prove that we put out screenshots [and videos] from both.

I'm sure we did a couple of PlayStation-exclusive content items; I'm positive we did. I know we did for *Prototype 2*. Both first parties are looking for some extra [content] for their platforms and we were always happy to oblige. I'm pretty sure we did a couple of more cosmetic changes for [PS3 and Xbox 360]. We made sure performance was equal for both, in order to treat all our fans equally and give them the best experience possible for the machine they're on.

Craddock: One piece of marketing people remember is Sucker Punch's interactions with Ben "Yahtzee" Croshaw, a game critic. How did that get started?

Chris Ansell: We did this hilarious drawing competition with Sucker Punch. One of the press issued a challenge: who could draw the opposing developer's hero in the most embarrassing light? Look up "Alex Mercer unicorn Sucker Punch." We loved that. We always talked very complementary about [Sucker Punch]. It's a talented studio, and *InFamous* is a fantastic game. I played the hell out of it. As we developed our social army for *Prototype*, we loved getting their opinions on *InFamous* so we could go out there and have a sort of friendly sparring match with anyone who was a PlayStation aficionado who loved *InFamous* because it was exclusive.

It was kind of nice to get *Prototype* involved in an online sparring match, which kind of was a proxy war for PlayStation versus Xbox gamers. It's an endless source of chatter, noise, and awareness, and if you can get your product into that loop, you get this free tidal wave of discussion because it's kind of a proxy for a bigger battle. That worked quite well. The same goes in reverse: you couldn't talk about *Prototype* without talking about *InFamous*. That was better for both of us. I liked that. It amplified the noise and people's awareness of *Prototype*. Otherwise they may have only been visiting PlayStation forums and never have heard about our game. Because of their closeness, people had to talk about both.

Craddock: Advertising for games during the Xbox 360 and PS3 generation seemed exciting to me as a consumer, because so many standards were changing. Social media was becoming a bigger part of consoles, as were tablets and smartphones for second-screen experiences, as they were called. What new tools did you harness to market *Prototype*?

Chris Ansell: An obvious one was Facebook and the use of Facebook for games marketing. We were really proud of the work we did in building up an army. We got to half a million followers without a dollar spent on any Facebook ads. I think that was also when the [advertisement] algorithm was a lot more friendly for getting the word out via organic posts. Now you have to pay for a lot more of that.

We were super proud of building up a fan base on Facebook. My plan is always to focus on the social media [platforms] you know you have a pattern for and you can deliver on, versus feeling you have to do all of them and you do many of them poorly. We focused on Facebook and certainly learned from our competitors, cherry-picking the good things we saw them doing and incorporated them into our plan as best practices.

The *Dead Space* guys had a great idea of doing a weekly, "Post your questions and we'll do a short video with the executive producer who will answer 10 of them." We did that with P1 and P2, and that was awesome. Just showing that you're listening, and proving you're listening to the community has incredible cumulative effects in terms of stickiness and them recommending friends to come in. Also, there was forum chatter about, "Wow, these devs actually get back to us. They listen." That's super important.

We were watching the emergence of this grassroots community back then in 2006, 2007. That was huge. The impact of things like Metacritic was growing. You had the emergence of sites like Kotaku, which were getting big audiences because of having raw, non-corporate, non-advertising-department-influenced writers. You had the emergence of these more aggressive, or honest blogs, which is great. Things were starting to change. You had to be more accurate; you had to be up front and honest with everybody in the community.

Craddock: What were some other considerations you had to keep in mind when working with those new tools?

Chris Ansell: There's no hiding. With the Internet and forums, and you had Justin.tv, which became Twitch, there was the start of, "There's no hiding. Let's just put everything out on the table and really invite the community in as part of the process." I think years before, you could very easily vanish and have a very controlled launch with a lot less transparency.

I think there's been more demand from gamers to want to see into the Willy Wonka chocolate factory so they can see how games are made and then make up their mind along that journey toward a purchase decision. We have the tools to show that to them now, but they were emerging back then. We were really excited to build the *Prototype* army up and show them inside the magic factory, get their opinions on things.

Obviously it takes a hell of a lot of time. You have opinions of all stripes on the Internet, and you can spin yourself in circles trying to satisfy the nine angry people as opposed to sticking to your vision. Those were some of the big changes there: bringing the community in and living via promises, explaining why you had to change things because the Internet has a great memory.

Craddock: How did you get press involved in promoting *Prototype*, besides offering preview and review copies?

Chris Ansell: Both factors [press and influencers] are super important. I think one helps the other. It's yin and yang; they impact each other for good and for bad, and both are super important. The press were incredibly influential and force multipliers. You could explain your vision to one person and then have a million people learn about it that day. That's very tough to do quickly and effectively through community unless you do the world's biggest Twitch stream.

I think that level of efficiency, speed, and planning that press offer product creators to get a message out will always be valuable. Being able to directly address your community as well, so that they feel listened to and informed about decisions, is obviously super important, too. I think both will always be very vital. Obviously we're seeing specific community members elevate and become influencers, the ultimate being when you get tens of millions of followers like PewDiePie. I've always seen that as just one piece of the puzzle.

Publications, blogs, podcasts… There are so many fantastic areas where we can connect with press and passionate people who have years of experience. We know that by going to press and to blog sites who have special interests, we can find a good home where those people will understand deep game systems and such instantly. It's helpful to maybe first introduce a concept with the press, and then you can go further into details with your community during community days and AMAs. But the structure that press provides will always be essential.

Craddock: What are some of your favorite memories from working on that project?

Chris Ansell: Working with the team. It was a crazy-talented team. Involving them in marketing and seeing the look on their face when we asked about assets to be made and giving them a say in them—that was very rewarding.

Also, just the look on press, retail buyers, internal teams, and management faces when we would reveal new demos, knowing that we had a real march on technology on Radical. When we could show people the density of open-world crowds, and what you could do with these calamitous physics interactions—watching their mouths gape was just so rewarding. It certainly makes a marketing job easier, and inspires you to think of more awesome storytelling assets and videos that you can create in this sandbox.

One idea we had, just because the physics allowed it, was there was a moment in one of the trailers where we thought, Goodness, do the helicopter rotors actually cut up zombies if you tilt the helicopter down toward the ground? And sure enough, they did. We put that in the end of one of the trailers to say, "Yes, you can even tilt helicopters to take out zombies just using the awesome tech." You were always discovering cool things in this sandbox. Showing that off and being so proud of the tech, knowing we had something great, was an incredible feeling.

Craddock: We talked about your favorite marketing materials from FF7, when you promoted it in Europe. Do you have any favorite materials from *Prototype*'s marketing?

Chris Ansell: We did a really kickass, VIP press kit. My colleague, Shamus Horak and I designed it. It was this dossier that we would give to third-party companies to partner with them; and to press. So many trailers. We worked with a wonderful trailer enemy called Stephen Rosenbaum. Stephen did some terrific trailers together with our in-house trailer editor Jim Carey; he was amazing. We produced a lot of trailers together and I'm really proud of all the trailers we did. That was a huge factor for our early hype, those killer trailers.

We did a lot of hilarious season things like April Fool's gags: "Take a look at Paper Airplane Man" video on YouTube. One of the programmers replaced the character with a paper airplane. He painted a face on it and made it look like it would be new DLC. It was called PAM: Paper Airplane Man. We did a fake cologne ad for *Prototype 2*. Take a look at the James Heller leather jacket replica. It cost a fortune, but it was epic. In the leather was embossed his tattoo that he has on his back. We did some Penny Arcade stuff that was really fun.

We started building the lore. One of the huge things that pulled me back into *World of WarCraft*, years after I'd worked on its marketing, was I loved buying the strategy guides because I loved reading the lore for the characters. That pulled me back into the game. Even as a gamer today, I was taking a look at Julian Gollop's *Phoenix Point*, a new version of *X-COM*. It was featured in *PC Gamer* recently. Their website right now is very [embryonic], but they made the time to create a section called Stories. The website basically consists of email signups and stories where they post lore and backstories.

It seems simple, but it's fantastic because it helps you invest and engages your imagination. Videos are great, but there's still an incredible pull toward the written word to fire people's imaginations. Story is most potent when it's in your head. Hitchcock says the secret to a good movie is "Script, script, script." it's the same for games.

That was my favorite ever job in the industry, working with Radical. It has such a nice place in my heart because building a new IP is the ultimate challenge for a marketer, especially in games. I had such a ball tackling that problem.

Exploring and fighting in *Prototype*.

Craddock:	Lindsey, Could you give an overview of your role as senior development director at Radical?
Lindsey Williamson Christy on Prototype:	I managed the budget, staffing and schedule for the team. I had a team of five Project Managers that would schedule various portions of the game and they would then all roll up into my master road map.
Craddock:	One of my goals with this article is to show how involved marketing teams can be—and perhaps must be—in a game's development. Did you work with Chris Ansell and/or others from marketing? If so, what did you collaborate on?
Lindsey Williamson Christy:	We worked very closely with Chris. He was a key member of the team, and *Prototype* was the first project where we had direct access to marking onsite at Radical. It was fantastic. I'm still friends with him to this day.
Craddock:	Leading up to their respective releases, many critics pointed out the similarities between *InFamous* and *Prototype*: super-powered antiheroes, ethical choices, open-world, parkour-style movement. How did you become aware of *InFamous* and its similarities to *Prototype*?

Lindsey Williamson Christy: I think we found out just before E3. We were a little worried at first, but then the more we saw of the game, the more we realized we were actually very different.

Craddock: You mentioned a "friendly rivalry" between Radical and Sucker Punch. How did that rivalry start?

Lindsey Williamson Christy: I think it started when Yahtzee first compared the two games. Before that we were vaguely aware of *InFamous* but not any more so than any other game that was slated to release at the same time.

Craddock: What form did that friendly rivalry take?

Lindsey Williamson Christy: I don't remember having any real contact with them at the time. A couple years some of the SEs on our team had moved on to work at Sucker Punch, I think one might still work there today.

Craddock: When two similar games launch, one sometimes cannibalizes the other. What were some of *Prototype*'s features that you wanted to highlight (in general, or in relation to *InFamous*) to set it apart? Or did *InFamous* not really affect how Radical presented *Prototype*?

Lindsey Williamson Christy: We honestly didn't really think that much about it. Our game was more visceral and more fluid in the locomotion system. I think we thought that was enough of a differentiation. Alex Mercer was unique in that he could morph parts of this body whereas *InFamous* was all about electricity.

Craddock: Chris Ansell said that one advantage of working on a product similar to someone else's is that no one can mention the competitor's product without also mentioning yours, and vice versa. Did you see that as an advantage? And do you think it worked in *Prototype*'s favor?

Lindsey Williamson Christy: I would agree with that, and I think it worked as we were on par with each other. It can be more challenging if one game clearly isn't of the same quality.

Craddock: I've often wondered if two developers working on similar games change their design, in big ways or small, because of something they noticed in the competitor's product. On that note, I've often wondered if triple-A schedules would even allow for something like that to happen! Speaking to *Prototype*, what were some of *InFamous*' features that interested you?

Lindsey Williamson Christy: We work in a bubble for so long, *Prototype* was in production for 30 months so our reaction time is very slow to any changes. Once your dev team gets on a path it's like turning the Titanic to make a change. I think we are all influenced by pop culture and the climate at the time of inception.

We were working on ten concepts initially. It got whittled down to three, and then *Prototype* came out as the winner. We started on it just after shipping *The Incredible Hulk: Ultimate Destruction* and had this great sandbox engine that's we'd been

	working on for about five years, so we were just looking for a game that could leverage all this tech.
Craddock:	Zero Punctuation reviewer Yahtzee, after joking that it was difficult to tell *InFamous'* and *Prototype's* protagonists apart, said he'd decide a winner based on which main character looked better in drag. Radical and SP participated. How did you become aware of that contest? What was your reaction to it?
Lindsey Williamson Christy:	I remember this really well, we had a lot of fun on the team. I wish I still had all the images that were created but never submitted.
Craddock:	What other moments from working on *Prototype* stand out to you?
Lindsey Williamson Christy:	It was the third game I made with the hairclub team and I'm super proud of it. It was a fantastic team and we worked really hard to get the game released. We went through two acquisitions during production on that game, so it was a bit tumultuous time for Radical. But the game team was just an amazing group of people. Getting the change to create an IP is rare and making a successful one is even more rare.

15

PowerUp Audio
Sound of Combat

Sound design is the sleeper MVP of the games industry. Horror games such as *Dead Space* and Capcom's 2019 remake of *Resident Evil 2* are gorgeous, but the sounds of groaning pipes and scuttling footsteps cement players in their settings, supplementing and enhancing art direction to make players more firmly believe in what they're seeing and doing.

Subset Games' turn-based strategy hit *Into the Breach* isn't a horror game, but sound still plays a big role in immersing the players in Subset's world of mechs and strategic terrain. PowerUp Audio shared the bulk of responsibility for creating the game's aural scene.

In early 2017, when *Into the Breach* was still in its earliest stages, I spoke with PowerUp co-founder and studio director Jeff Tangsoc, fellow co-founder and creative director Kevin Regamey, and lead sound designer Joey Godard about their work on the game.

**

Craddock:	What led you to form PowerUp Audio?
Jeff Tangsoc:	We worked at a previous game audio house and were assigned games that we weren't necessarily interested in. So the work was there and we were gaining tons of experience in a variety of different titles, but we didn't feel passionate about the work itself. We decided to form PowerUp Audio to bring our experience and passion together—to work on games we would play ourselves, and would be proud to show our peers and ourselves.
Kevin Regamey:	Jeff and I used to work at another guns-for-hire style game audio studio. While there, we worked on a ton of projects and acquired some great working experience, but unfortunately the studio was first and foremost a product-based content creation kind of business. We as employees were kept at a considerable distance from the actual developers with whom we were

working, and were never really given a chance to actively sink our teeth into a project further than simply "making the sounds."

We both quit after three or four years of working there, and formed PowerUp Audio shortly thereafter. Now we're far more involved in the process of making games, and much happier with our jobs.

Craddock: How did you meet the guys at Subset Games?

Kevin Regamey: As is common, we met Justin from Subset at the Game Developers Conference in San Francisco. It's a few years back now…but I think we happened to be playing some games together at an industry party.

Jeff Tangsoc: We met probably two years ago. The indie community is surprisingly small, with many of the same indie devs [traveling] in the same parties, meetups, and events.

Craddock: What is PUA's collaborative process with developers, as it pertains to Subset Games and their game *Into the Breach*?

Jeff Tangsoc: We are adamant in not just being a vendor in the process of game design. We want to be as much of a team member as possible. So we eschew the "send a zip file along with an invoice" type of contracting. Since we work remotely from Subset, we ask them for repository access, meaning that we are able to insert our work directly into the game-in-progress via internet connection.

We are able to play the latest builds of the game this way. We also work with audio middleware, FMOD, meaning that we work within a sound-designer-friendly program that hooks to Subset's code with minimal interference on both ends. Highly recommended for any sound designer looking take full onus of their work—from asset creation, to implementation, to mix and play-testing.

We play as much of game-in-progress as possible and create a spreadsheet of sounds with think are needed in the game. Subset adds and edits this list as to make it the most definitive document for what needs to be in the game sound wise. We also assist in music implementation, so Ben composes the tracks, and we put it in the game for him and mix it relative to our sound effects, and trigger it to his specifications.

Kevin Regamey: Our general aim these days is to help out on projects however we can. Typically that's in regards to sound design, music, and voiceover, but it's common for us to contribute in other ways such as playtesting, marketing, design input, or helping at PAX booths. Occasionally we'll even be the ones setting the developer high-scores for our players to beat.

Into the Breach by Subset Games.

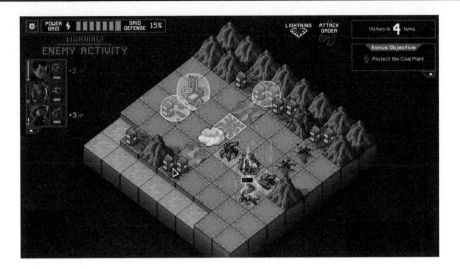

Craddock: Could you tell me about some of the audio you've done for *Into the Breach* and what the production process was like? From conception to final-ish product. ("Ish" because *Into the Breach* isn't finished yet, of course.)

Jeff Tangsoc: Subset created a debug map of sorts that allowed us to access all of the game assets thus far. We identify which sounds need to be made for each mech, enemy, environment, skill, and UI. Creatively, we discuss with Subset on what they are looking for: how audio can be showcased in certain events, or how audio can help bolster certain visuals, or how our audio can help accentuate some music tracks.

    Then we set off either recording sound effects, using libraries and processing the effects, or creating sound effects from scratch via synthesis. Our work is passed on internally first, as to give our team a sense of cohesion in what we are aiming for. After internal approval, it goes in the game for Subset to playtest and provide their thoughts.

Joey Godard: *Into the Breach* has such a strong visual aesthetic and consistent gameplay mechanics, so while we still have lots of sound work to do on the game, establishing the overall tone for the soundscape came pretty naturally. We're using synths to create UI sounds that are digital and light in the menus, and heavier while navigating to provide grounded movement as you move across the world and in to each combat grid.

    We knew we wanted to fill out the world as much as possible, so we thought realistic background ambiences would help sell the environments and provide a welcome contrast to Justin's pixel art.

    The most difficult part so far is probably the units themselves. Although they appear small in game, you have to imagine them as massive mechs and monsters the size of the buildings that surround them. The game also doesn't make you wait; it's fast paced and units move across the grid very quickly. Finding a way to both give weight and size to them, and also an individual identity is challenging.

Each sound has to be large and tight, almost like a drum beat. I think we're getting there.

Into the Breach.

Craddock: What sorts of resources does Subset Games provide to help you and your team create the right type of audio for a particular unit, character, etc.? For example, do they send concept artwork or playable builds of the game?

Jeff Tangsoc: The repository has everything we need to find out what is in the game. We use Google Docs to create spreadsheets that track which art/animation assets are ready to have audio for, and also keep track of what sounds we've designed already. We use Slack for real-time conversations ranging from creative talks, technical implementation, and scheduling.

Joey Godard: Justin and Matt have been great. We have access to an up-to-date build which we can connect to with middleware (FMOD in our case). Hearing your newest work quickly and being able to mix on the fly is how any sound designer wants to work.

                 They're also very receptive to any of our ideas and also provide immediate detailed feedback on anything new that we do. On top of that, Ben's music is a great source of inspiration and direction. We've worked with Ben on other games already (*StarCrawlers*, *Skytorn*), so we knew that finding a balance between music and sound would come quickly and effortlessly.

Craddock: Do you have a particular piece of work for *Into the Breach* that stands out to you?

| Jeff Tangsoc: | I'm a huge fan of the UI so far in the game. Subset's aesthetic is very clean and distilled. Super easy to read. The audio should reflect that: accessing certain information in a heavily menu based game should feel seamless, effortless. At the same time, the world we are creating is not "clean sci-fi," like how the Enterprise looks or a futuristic city from Guardians of the Galaxy. |

It's apocalyptic. The mechs are state of the art but still feel grounded in reality. We had to find a careful balance between futuristic sound effects that would still sound at home in the realm of a sonar ping.

| Craddock: | Since *Into the Breach* is still a work in progress, when do you consider a piece of audio finished? Or is everything still in flux? |

| Jeff Tangsoc: | Everything is still in flux up until we reach a content complete stage. Even then, other factors, like music direction, still need to be considered before we finalize our sound effects for release. |

| Kevin Regamey: | It's true that everything we create is up for reconsideration until we ship a game. Sometimes even after. In any creative field it can be challenging to call something "done," but generally if a piece of audio we've created is serving the creative direction, serving its purpose in terms of design, and sounds rad, we're good to ship it. |

| Craddock: | What items are on your immediate agenda for *Into the Breach*? |

| Jeff Tangsoc: | General content creation, music editing, implementation, possible voice acting, and filling out the non-*battlefield* elements to create as immersive of a world as we can. |

| Kevin Regamey: | Playing more. It's…it's really fun. |

16

S. D. Perry—Author

Most gamers loathe game-to-movie adaptations, and for good reason. Directors rarely treat source material with the reverence it deserves, resulting in movies so bad even diehard fans of the games that influenced them refuse to acknowledge the silver-screen adaptations.

Game-to-book adaptations are a different beast. Just like bookworms who squirm and sizzle when TV and movie adaptations of their favorite yarns dare to stray from the book, gamers want to see their favorite scenes and characters play out on the page exactly as they did on their consoles and PCs. Yet there's a balancing act of which many readers are not aware. Jane Jensen's novelization of the first Gabriel Knight game, penned by the game designer herself, was almost a one-to-one recreation of the game, resulting in puzzles and sequences that felt bogged down. Some things work better in one medium than another.

To fans of *Resident Evil*, Stephani Danelle "S. D." Perry proved herself as an author capable of determining what elements of Capcom's survival-horror series worked on the page, what needed to go, and what needed a makeover. Perry wrote seven novels in total—five that covered game stories such as *Resident Evil 2*, and *Resident Evil – Code: Veronica*, and two that came straight from the author's imagination.

As a huge fan of the novels, I was honored when S. D. Perry (do not call her Stephani!) accepted my request to answer some of my questions about her *Resident Evil* books, her writing career, and the trials and tribulations of adapting animated pictures to strings of words.

**

Craddock:	What led you on the path to writing? Was writing full-time something you wanted to do, or did you stumble upon it by accident?
S. D. Perry:	I started keeping a journal when I was 10, so I grew up feeling comfortable writing. My father is a writer, too, so I always felt like it was a job possibility. I started writing poetry and stories when I was a teen and my dad would tell me to send them out, try to sell them. So I kind of fell into it, but I also had a lot of practice and encouragement early on.
Craddock:	How has your dad influenced your writing?

Perry: I don't think I would have become a writer if my father wasn't one. When I was in my early 20s, he offered to collaborate with me so I could get money for school. We did two books together and my career (such as it is) took off from there. He also taught me how to write action.

Craddock: Do you play many video games? How would you describe your level of interest in the gaming scene?

Perry: I played a lot in my 20s and 30s. At the ripe old age of 45, with two kids in the house, I usually have other stuff to do. I play apps on my phone, mostly. Boring, but easy to put down. My sons are the gamers.

Craddock: You've written several tie-in novels over the course of your career, and not just for Capcom's *Resident Evil* games. How did you get started in the tie-in space?

Perry: Props to my dad. He wrote tie-ins, and offered to share a byline with me on an *Aliens* book, for Dark Horse Comics. We did two of them, and then I started doing my own tie-ins—a couple of movie novelizations, more *Aliens* stuff, then into RE and *Star Trek*, among others.

Craddock: One assumes that tie-in novels could prove critical to helping an author gain exposure, since consumers are already very familiar with the tie-in property, such as *Resident Evil* and *Aliens*. Did you find that to be the case with your work?

Perry: I've written tie-ins/novelizations for my whole career, so my fans are usually fans of those franchises. Have I gained exposure? I wouldn't say I'm famous. *Resident Evil* and *Aliens* and *Star Trek* are famous. I'm just a semi-talented *hack*.

Craddock: Without getting into specific numbers, how well did tie-in novels pay when you wrote the *Resident Evil* and *Aliens* books? Does that market still pay about the same, or has it gotten better or worse?

Perry: I wrote all those books for a flat up-front fee and occasionally a percent of a percent of royalties; that's usually how it is when you're writing in someone else's universe. I was offered between $8,000 and $12,000 per book. So I got paid to write them, and if they did well, I sometimes saw a few hundred dollars here or there later on. The RE books definitely had the best royalties, but they dried up years ago. When the series was reissued a few years back—by a different company, which had leased the publishing rights—no one even told me.

I have no idea what the market pays now. For writers in my bracket, $8k–$12k is still pretty good, I think. That's about what I got on my last big project, a year ago. I know that the bigger franchises—*Star Wars*, for instance—pay a lot more.

Craddock: What do you enjoy most about writing tie-in novels? What do you enjoy least?

Perry: I most enjoy trying to capture the flavor of the property—the game, comic, script—and put it into words. I mean, the stuff I write about has fans for a reason. I consider it part of my job to find that reason and write as a fan. I like working with characters that someone else has created, trying to keep them consistent; it's a challenge, which is fun.

Least? Tight deadlines. And lack of serious royalties. But that's the nature of contract work.

Craddock:	How familiar were you with *Resident Evil* before writing the books?
Perry:	Only the first game was out when I was first contacted; the second was about to be released. I had gotten the game months after it came out, and was still in the mansion trying to kill the giant snake when I got the call.
Craddock:	How did you get the opportunity to adapt the games to novels?
Perry:	A bright young editor at Simon & Schuster had gotten the publishing rights for *Resident Evil* and was looking for someone to do a few books. He contacted my dad, first. My father was busy, but mentioned that his daughter was a fan of the game and had published tie-ins. The bright young editor—Marco Palmieri—contacted me, and I said heck yeah.
Craddock:	Before you started, what guidelines did Capcom set down? For example, were you required to work with certain page counts? Did Capcom mandate that certain events take place?
Perry:	Capcom had very little involvement in the books, and only ever contacted my editor. In the initial pitch, I'd done some backstory on the mansion, and they asked me to leave it out because they had their own backstory. Other than that, I don't believe they had much to say.
Craddock:	In *Resident Evil: City of the Dead*, which follows the events of *Resident Evil 2*, you had Ada Wong find the heart key hidden in the statue located in the RCPD lobby, rather than have Leon or Claire search it out. How much creative control did you have in choosing which in-game events to adapt exactly as they occurred, versus which ones you had to cut (such as the "push the bookshelves around" puzzle in the library of RE2) or alter?
Perry:	If I'd just novelized the games, I would have had 300 pages of the same two characters running back and forth to solve puzzles. I had to have creative license to move the story along, and give the other characters something to do. I had pretty much complete control over the decisions; my editor was happy as long as I was including the bigger puzzles and keeping it entertaining.
Craddock:	Regarding creative control, how much say did you have in each book? I imagine that, when adapting one of the games, your parameters were well-defined: this is how the game starts, and this is where it ends.
Perry:	I wasn't given a whole lot of direction. This was back in the mid-'90s, and video game novelizations weren't all that big yet. So I winged it. I did it the way a fan would, the way anyone would—followed the events as they happened and told the story that went along with it. My editor added some stuff in—the mysterious Trent was his idea, for example—but I did the rest.
Craddock:	Did Capcom provide any materials for you to reference while writing? For instance, you did a great job recreating many iconic environments such as the police station in RE2 and the Spencer Estate in RE1. Did you have screenshots or other documents to reference when describing those areas?
Perry:	They sent me a few character shots for the second game. Other than that, the only reference materials I got were game guides, from my editor. For the first game, I just played it every time I had a question about some detail. By the time I finished the book, I could complete the whole game in less than two

Craddock: hours. For me, that was an achievement. I also used the VCR to record the game while I played, so I could find what I needed for a given scene.

Craddock: The second and fourth books in your series—*Caliban Cove* and *Underworld*, respectively—were unique stories never before told in the RE universe. Did Capcom supply outlines for those, or did you come up with the premise yourself?

Perry: Those were me. I pitched them to my editor and he said go for it.

Craddock: One aspect I loved about the RE books was that you took the time to flesh out non-playable characters (NPCs) such as Chief Irons and Annette Birkin from *Resident Evil 2*. Was it your choice to write from the perspectives of those characters, or did Capcom ask you to do that?

Perry: Capcom really wasn't involved. Like I said earlier, I had to fill pages with more than just solving puzzles, so I used the non-POV characters to move the story along. And thanks! I'm glad you liked it!

Craddock: Walk us through the process of writing one of the RE novels. Let's start with the first book, *The Umbrella Conspiracy*, which follows the original *Resident Evil*. What was the starting point? What came next? What steps followed and led up to finishing the book and seeing it appear in stores?

Perry: I agreed to write four books: two based on the first two games, two original set in the same universe. I wrote one at a time, and as I turned each one in, my editor would ask for changes. I rewrote until he was happy (or at least not unhappy!). He sent each to Capcom, they were okayed with minor corrections. Galleys were sent out for final corrections, then the book went to press, then it came out.

Craddock: In RE games, players find progressively stronger weapons, such as the shotgun and the bazooka, to even the playing field against tougher enemies. In your books, the characters tend to find fewer weapons, and are constantly in danger of running low on supplies. I really like this wrinkle; it adds tension. Was it your call to steer the characters off the video game-y path of finding increasingly powerful weapons in order to create a tenser, more survival-driven atmosphere?

Perry: Yes, it was my call... And yes! Plus, having awesome weapons and endless ammo in real life leads to practical issues; like, who wants to run through a house of horror lugging a bazooka and 40 pounds of ammo?

Craddock: You might remember from playing *Resident Evil* that the game's tone and dialogue were. less than serious, one could say. One might go so far as to describe them as "cheesy." You took a much darker, more serious tone in your books. Was it your goal to intentionally steer clear of cheesiness?

Perry: Yes, and my editor agreed. The voice acting was silly, and we went into the project looking to make it seem real. I mean, obviously it's fiction, but I don't think I would have enjoyed writing tongue-in-cheek... And I don't think the fans would have dug it, either.

Craddock: Every writer practices unique techniques, disciplines, and schedules. How would you describe your approach to writing as you wrote the RE novels? Did that approach change from first draft to second, third, and so on? For example, many authors stress that the first draft is all about dumping words on paper; that's the hard part. Then you go back and rewrite, polish, rewrite, polish.

Perry: This is a bit embarrassing to admit, although anyone reading the stories closely has probably noticed… I did all of those books first draft. I got it on paper, I did one read through for typos, I sent it off. The deadlines were very tight—a month to six weeks per book—and I put off working until I had to do like 20 pages a day, so there wasn't time for extensive rewrites. Looking back, I wish I had taken more time to craft and polish, but I was young and inexperienced and I thought I could pull it off.

I was so late on each deadline that my poor editor was mostly stuck with what I sent him. I'd like to think that the books worked because I'm incredibly talented and work best under stress, but honestly, I was lucky; the material was all there, I just had to fill in the blanks. Only my editor had contact with them [Capcom]. He kind of intimated to me that Capcom didn't even like the books that much, although to be honest, I don't remember. This was all 20 years ago. My editor asked me to make changes here and there, to keep stuff entertaining. Capcom's only issue was with some stuff I'd made up about the Spencer Estate, early in the first book.

Craddock: As with the games, your *Resident Evil 0* novelization came up several years after the first three games in the series. How did you get the chance to backtrack in the timeline and write the *Resident Evil 0* book?

Perry: The first four books did well, and Simon & Schuster still had the rights, so I was hired to adapt the next games. I think that's when I started adding in that disclaimer at the front of books, about how the games and books were coming out at different times so probably wouldn't be consistent. Capcom didn't refer to the books when they were making their games, or give me any inside information on their future plans; I had to either come up with an explanation for the differences or just ignore timeline issues. Mostly, I just tried to adapt what was in front of me.

Craddock: I'm disappointed that we haven't seen novelizations for *Resident Evil 4* or other later games. Did Capcom approach you with plans to adapt RE4 or any games that followed?

Perry: Nope. Someone else leased the publishing rights. I was contacted by a nice editor at another house about eight years ago about maybe doing more, but apparently Capcom decided to stop publishing just about then. Again, I got the impression that they weren't fans of the books, but maybe that's just me.

Craddock: Which of the *Resident Evil* novels was your favorite to write?

Perry: *Caliban Cove*, because I got to have a character bite and eat someone's face.

Craddock: Which of the RE novels gave you the most trouble?

Perry: *City of the Dead*, because there was just so much material.

Craddock: Which character was your favorite to write for?

Perry: Probably Rebecca [Chambers]; she was such a good girl.

Craddock: Which scenes from any of the RE books stand out to you?

Perry: Hmm… I wrote them all in such a rush, I was always late on those books; mostly I remember trying to come up with synonyms for gore. I remember the crow puzzle and the giant spiders, I remember an underwater lab and the Licker and a train crash and the Antarctic and a submarine. It all blends together; I wrote them fast, and haven't gone back to read them in a very long time.

Craddock: If you could go back, is there anything you would change about any of the RE books?

Perry: Yes. I'd get rid of a lot of clichés that I used because I was still a very young writer and I would finally correct my gun ignorance. When I wrote those, I thought "clip" and "Magazine" were interchangeable. I'm sure I made lots of mistakes.

Craddock: What are you up to these days? Any books in the works?

Perry: Let's see. An *Aliens* project I worked on just came out: *The Weyland-Yutani Report*; I have a zombie short story coming out next month in an anthology, *SNAFU: Survival of the Fittest*, and a pop-up book (not for kids!) coming out in October. I just turned in a story for another anthology, and am finishing a second original novel, a haunted house book.

      Oh, and I also just signed a contract for a thing I can't talk about yet, but it'll make RE fans happy—think action and guts. One of these days, I'll make a website so I can announce stuff to people.

Index

Page numbers in *italic* indicate illustration.